MW01278484

Chronic Fatigue Syndrome: CDC and NIH Research Activities

United States Government Accountability Office
Health, Education, and Human Services Division

United States General Accounting Office

GAO

Report to the Honorable
Harry Reid, U.S. Senate

ıne 2000

CHRONIC FATIGUE SYNDROME

CDC and NIH Research Activities Are Diverse, but Agency Coordination Is Limited

GAO
Accountability ★ Integrity ★ Reliability

O/HEHS-00-98

Contents

Letter   3

Appendixes

Appendix I: Background on Chronic Fatigue Syndrome   30

Appendix II: Accounting Issues at CDC   34

Appendix III: CDC Research Efforts and Publications   37

Appendix IV: NIH Research Efforts and Grants   44

Appendix V: Congressionally Requested CFS Activities for CDC
                and NIH   54

Appendix VI: External Review Recommendations to CDC and NIH   59

Appendix VII: NIH Expenditures on CFS Research, by Institute and
                Center   64

Appendix VIII: NIH Activities in Support of CFS Research   65

Appendix IX: Comments From the Department of Health and
                Human Services   69

Tables

Table 1:   U.S. Studies of CFS Prevalence Based on Clinical
           Evaluation of Samples of Local Populations   32

Table 2:   NIH Disposition of Projects Identified by CRISP From 1997
           Through 1999 Not Included in NIH's List   47

Table 3:   NIH-Funded R01 (Research Project) Grants Related to CFS   48

Table 4:   NIH-Funded Intramural Research Projects Related to CFS   49

Table 5:   NIH-Funded Grants and Projects Not Including R01
           (Research Project) Grants and Intramural Projects Related
           to CFS   50

Table 6:   NIAID Cooperative Research Center Projects Related to
           CFS   52

Table 7:   Congressionally Requested CFS Activities for CDC   54

Table 8:   Congressionally Requested CFS Activities for NIH   57

Table 9:   Recommendations From CDC's 1996 Peer Review and
           Agency Response   59

Table 10: Recommendations From CDC's 1999 Peer Review, Board of
           Scientific Counselor Review, and Meeting With Patient
           Advocates, and Agency Response   61

Figures

Figure 1: CDC Funding, Fiscal Years 1988 Through 1999   1
Figure 2: NIH Expenditures, Fiscal Years 1988 Through 1999   1
Figure 3: Proportion of CFS Funds Retained at Each Level of
           CDC, Fiscal Years 1998 Through 1999   1
Figure 4: CDC Publications   3

Abbreviations

CDC	Centers for Disease Control and Prevention
CFS	chronic fatigue syndrome
CFSCC	CFS Coordinating Committee
CRISP	Computer Retrieval of Information on Scientific Projects
FDA	Food and Drug Administration
HHS	Department of Health and Human Services
NCI	National Cancer Institute
NCRR	National Center for Research Resources
NHLBI	National Heart, Lung, and Blood Institute
NIAID	National Institute of Allergy and Infectious Diseases
NIAMS	National Institute of Arthritis and Musculoskeletal and Skin Diseases
NICHD	National Institute of Child Health and Human Development
NIH	National Institutes of Health
NIMH	National Institute of Mental Health
NINDS	National Institute of Neurological Disorders and Stroke

GAO

Accountability * Integrity * Reliability

United States General Accounting Office
Washington, D.C. 20548

Health, Education, and
Human Services

B-283171

June 2, 2000

The Honorable Harry Reid
United States Senate

Dear Senator Reid:

Chronic fatigue syndrome (CFS) is a debilitating and complex disorder that potentially affects more than 800,000 Americans—yet it has no known cause or cure. CFS is defined by profound fatigue that is not improved by bed rest and other symptoms, such as weakness, muscle pain, cognitive difficulties, and problems with sleep. CFS is diagnosed only by excluding other possible causes of the fatigue and only after the fatigue has persisted for at least 6 months.

Since fiscal year 1988, congressional appropriations committee reports have asked the Centers for Disease Control and Prevention (CDC) and the National Institutes of Health (NIH) to initiate investigations and projects related to CFS, a disorder each agency began investigating in the mid-1980s. The goals of their work have included defining CFS and determining its prevalence and cause or causes. CDC and NIH research to date has focused largely on estimating prevalence, investigating suspected clusters of CFS, and examining possible causes. In 1996, the Secretary of the Department of Health and Human Services (HHS) established a committee of representatives from CDC, NIH, and other federal agencies; scientists; and patient advocates largely for the purpose of coordinating federal research efforts on CFS.

Since fiscal year 1987, NIH has devoted approximately $57.6 million to the study of CFS through intramural and extramural CFS grants. The committee reports indicated a level of funding to support CFS work at CDC totaling $44.7 million through fiscal year 1998.[1] For fiscal years 1995 through 1998, the committees recommended that CDC spend $23.4 million on the study of CFS. However, in 1999, the Inspector General of HHS reported that CDC had expended $8.8 million on activities unrelated to CFS and $4.1 million on inadequately documented indirect costs—as much as half of the funds the committees recommended for CFS. Because of concerns related to the redirection of CFS funds at CDC and questions raised by patient advocates about the lack of research progress, you asked us to (1) identify the CFS research activities that CDC and NIH have supported, (2) determine the funds and resources CDC and NIH have devoted to CFS research, and (3) describe how CDC and NIH coordinate research and involve patient organizations and external researchers in developing their CFS research programs.

For this study, we reviewed documents from CDC and NIH and talked with agency officials; reviewed minutes of and attended meetings of HHS' CFS Coordinating Committee (CFSCC); and talked with current and past federal, patient advocate, and scientific members of the chartered committee. We reviewed work in the years that each agency devoted funding to CFS research: for CDC, fiscal years 1988 through 1999; for NIH, fiscal years 1987 through 1999. We did not evaluate the quality of the research conducted. We conducted our work between July 1999 and May 2000 in accordance with generally accepted government auditing standards.

Results in Brief

For approximately the last 12 years, both CDC and NIH have conducted broad range of activities related to CFS. CDC has focused largely on prevalence and disease causes, including the search for infectious and immunological abnormalities. NIH has focused primarily on CFS' effects bodily systems and possible causal agents. Both agencies' work has generally been consistent with their missions, and both have initiated me

---

[1]The Congress did not make a line item appropriation to the CFS program. Rather, the appropriations committees expressed their funding expectations for the CFS program in reports that accompanied the annual "lump sum" appropriation to CDC. See, for example H.R. Rep. No. 103-156, at 44 (1994); S. Rep. No. 103-143, at 69 (1994); and H.R. Conf. Rep. 105-825, at 1270 (1998). Because the Congress did not use a line item appropriation to fund the CFS program, the CDC director had latitude in determining whether funds would be allocated in strict accordance with the CFS program funding guidance expressed by the Congress.

of the projects that have been requested in appropriations report language and the projects defined in their program plans.

Funds for CFS research have increased at both CDC and NIH since 1987. Much of the increase occurred in the first few years; over the past 4 years, funds have generally not increased. At CDC, the lengthy and uncertain process for allocating CFS funds to the branch responsible for most of the CFS work has resulted in delays in undertaking particular projects. Further, CDC's redirection of funds has resulted in reductions in CFS resources that have impeded the agency's CFS research. However, CDC has begun a process to restore all redirected CFS funds. NIH has taken a number of steps to facilitate the funding of CFS projects, including issuing program announcements, establishing a special emphasis panel to review CFS grant applications, and using a discretionary program to fund additional studies. NIH has also supported a number of research centers on CFS.

Coordination between CDC and NIH and their use of input from external researchers and patient advocates in developing agency research programs have been limited. CDC and NIH have not jointly conducted research, although CDC's advisory panel and external peer reviewers have recommended that CDC undertake such a collaboration. CFSCC, chartered to encourage federal coordination, has helped to facilitate some interagency communication, but it has not provided an effective forum for developing coordinated research programs. Certain shortcomings in how CFSCC conducts its work may have limited its usefulness, although the committee has made recent efforts to improve its effectiveness.

HHS commented on a draft of this report and generally agreed with our findings, particularly that CFSCC could be more effective.

Background

Because there is currently no known biological way to differentiate cases of CFS from other conditions, researchers use clinical descriptions of symptoms to define CFS. To date, CFS has had two different case definitions. The first case definition, developed in 1988, required that, in addition to fatigue, patients had to meet 8 of 14 symptom or physical criteria. In 1994, the definition was revised to include only four of eight symptoms in addition to fatigue. An additional revision of the case definition is being considered. In addition, other terms have been used to describe the illness—such as chronic fatigue and immune dysfunction syndrome and myalgic encephalomyelitis—and other definitions of CFS are used in other countries. Estimates of CFS prevalence in the United

States have varied from 2.0 to 7.3 per 100,000 under the first definition to 238 to 422 per 100,000 under the revised case definition. This last estimate translates to about 836,000 Americans. (For a more detailed discussion of CFS case definition, prevalence estimates, and research on possible causes, see app. I.)

Evidence to support many of the hypothesized causes of CFS has been insufficient, but other hypotheses continue to be developed. And while CFS has no known cause or cure, there are some therapies for CFS that are directed at relieving patient symptoms.[2]

Federal CFS Research Through CDC and NIH

CDC's CFS work is performed largely in the Viral Exanthems and Herpesvirus Branch within the Division of Viral and Rickettsial Diseases under the National Center for Infectious Diseases. CFS work is assigned to this branch because early hypotheses about the causes of CFS included viruses covered by the branch, such as Epstein-Barr virus and herpes viruses. CDC allocates funds budgeted for CFS to the branch through the center and the division. Annually, each branch of the Division of Viral and Rickettsial Diseases presents a review of its program activities, plans, and accomplishments. Most of CDC's CFS research is conducted extramurally, primarily through research contracts. Intramural work is planned by individual branch chiefs and reported in these reviews as part of the branches' plans. In 1998, it was alleged that in fiscal years 1995 through 1998, CDC had spent funds that had been budgeted for CFS on other programs and had misled the Congress about how it had spent these funds. At CDC's request, HHS' Inspector General conducted an audit of the CFS program for these years and found that about one-third of the funds ($8.8 million) had been spent on non-CFS-related activities. An additional one-fifth ($4.1 million) of funds were indirect costs not adequately documented to determine applicability to CFS. While the Inspector General noted that CDC was not legally prohibited from spending funds this way, the Inspector General found that these discrepancies resulted from deficiencies in CDC's internal control system for handling direct and indirect costs. (See app. II.)

---

[2]These have included pharmacological therapies, such as medications to improve sleep or relieve pain, and nonpharmacological therapies, such as acupuncture, chiropractic manipulation, massage, and yoga. Certain psychotherapies, such as cognitive behavior therapy, have also been used in efforts to help patients cope and alleviate some of the symptoms associated with CFS. In addition, some consider that modest regular exercise to avoid deconditioning is important.

NIH's CFS research is conducted by both intramural scientists employed by NIH as well as extramural scientists who are awarded grants or contracts for their work. The largest portion of NIH's CFS work has been performed within the National Institute of Allergy and Infectious Diseases (NIAID). Other NIH institutes and centers that have funded CFS research include the National Institute of Mental Health; the National Institute of Neurological Disorders and Stroke; the National Center for Research Resources; the National Cancer Institute; the National Heart, Lung, and Blood Institute; the National Institute of Arthritis and Musculoskeletal and Skin Diseases; and the National Institute on Child Health and Human Development. Four additional NIH institutes and centers have joined the solicitation for grant applications for work on CFS; but, to date, none have been funded by these units.[3] External grant applications are reviewed by special emphasis panels of external scientists who rate the merit of each application. Final decisions about the merit of grants are subsequently made by the relevant institute's external advisory council, which meets three times each year. Every 4 years, each laboratory in the intramural research program is reviewed by its institute's board of scientific counselors. Recently, NIH moved the responsibility for coordinating efforts on CFS from NIAID to the Office of the NIH Director. NIH officials told us this was to centralize these efforts at NIH.

Role of CFSCC

To help ensure coordination of federal research efforts related to CFS, HHS' Assistant Secretary for Health in 1990 assembled a group of federal researchers—adding nonfederal scientists and patient advocates as consultants in 1994—to form an interagency committee. Then in 1996, the Secretary of HHS chartered CFSCC, in part, to ensure coordination and communication regarding CFS. The committee consists of seven members, appointed by the Secretary, and five ex-officio members. Of the seven appointed members, three are biomedical research scientists; two have expertise in health care services or disability issues or represent private health care services insurers; and two represent voluntary organizations that serve people with CFS. Members are invited to serve for overlapping 4-year terms. The ex-officio members are representatives from CDC, NIH, the Food and Drug Administration (FDA), the Health Resources and Services

---

[3]The four additional institutes and centers are the National Institute of Environmental Health Sciences, the National Institute of Nursing Research, the National Institute of Diabetes and Digestive and Kidney Diseases, and the Office on Research on Women's Health.

Administration, and the Social Security Administration.[4] The Assistant Secretary for Health chairs the committee. CFSCC management and support services are provided on a 2-year rotating basis between NIH and CDC, and the ex-officio representative from that agency serves as cochai Meetings are held approximately two times a year and are open to the public.

CFSCC membership is different from that of all other HHS advisory committees. For nearly all of HHS' 12 other similar advisory committees, the federal members serve in an ex-officio capacity and are nonvoting. CFSCC is the only committee chaired by federal representatives when there are nonfederal members of the committee. All other committees wi nonfederal members have a nonfederal member as the chair of the committee.

CDC and NIH Research Activities Are Diverse

While researchers and advocates have expressed concerns about the breadth of CFS research at CDC and NIH, we found the agencies have conducted a broad range of activities related to CFS. The agencies have also undertaken efforts to educate patients and physicians. These activiti and efforts have generally been consistent with what would be expected based on the agencies' mission statements. Further, both agencies initiat the majority of studies and activities that were requested in appropriatio committee reports. Finally, the agencies generally conducted activities mentioned in their own program plans and responded to recommendatio of external expert reviewers.

CDC and NIH Conduct a Broad Range of CFS Activities Consistent With Their Missions

CDC has conducted activities in most areas of its recent mission statements for its CFS program. For example, CDC has led efforts to develop a rigorous case definition for CFS, which is necessary to evalua whether CFS is a single disease or a set of symptoms that could have multiple causes. The agency has also conducted a number of surveillanc studies to determine the prevalence of CFS, starting with a study using

---

[4]Federal agencies other than CDC and NIH have the following roles related to CFS: new CFS-related products or advertising require review by FDA; the Health Resources and Services Administration generally translates research findings into practice and address issues related to the training of health professionals; and the Social Security Administra tracks medicine and science behind disorders like CFS so that their policies reflect the clinical world, especially related to rulings on CFS disability claims.

physician referrals to identify possible CFS patients and later shifting to a more active community-based approach. In addition, CDC has examined a number of possible CFS risk factors, including viral and immunological ones, and has relied on data collected from its surveillance studies to describe the natural history of CFS. To date, however, the agency has not identified any cause or causes for CFS.

As part of its CFS mission, CDC has also undertaken a variety of efforts to educate practitioners, professionals, and the public, including scientific publications, a web site, a toll-free hot line, and a booklet about CFS. Because there have been so few objective findings to date, it has not been possible for CDC to develop control strategies. (See app. III for more details on CDC's research efforts and a list of its CFS-related publications.)

With CDC's direction of an additional $12.9 million to its CFS program over 4 years—to compensate for redirected funds in prior years—work has been planned in a number of additional areas, including a national survey to estimate prevalence, a national patient registry, a workshop to determine if the current case definition for CFS should be revised, endocrine and sleep studies, and genetic tests of tissue samples. For example, in May 2000, CDC held a 3-day workshop to assess current clinical and empirical knowledge concerning the definition of CFS. Participants agreed that it was premature to revise the case definition and that future revisions should be based on data-driven research rather than consensus clinical opinion.

While CDC has conducted research in a broad range of areas, the agency has been criticized by researchers and patient advocates about the lack of openness of its efforts. For example, because CDC sometimes does not release findings from its studies until they are published in a professional journal, the latest information may not always be immediately available. However, this is a common practice among scientific researchers, and obtaining peer review prior to publication is used to ensure the integrity of the communication. Further, CDC officials reported that the agency follows its normal procedures in releasing results of its CFS studies. We also found that CDC has periodically presented preliminary results from its surveillance studies at scientific conferences and regularly reviews the current status of its research at CFSCC meetings.

Within NIH, NIAID's intramural and extramural research programs have been responsible for most of NIH's work on CFS, and the institute has supported work on causes, prevalence, origin and development of diseases, diagnosis, and treatment. NIH has funded investigations of a number of possible causes, including immunologic, neuropsychologic, neuroendocrinologic, brain wave, and infectious aspects of CFS. However NIH, like CDC, has not yet been able to identify a single cause or group of causes for CFS. NIAID has supported a number of attempts to estimate the prevalence of CFS, particularly a large epidemiological project in Chicago to study the socioeconomic and ethnic variability of CFS. Early work to identify the origin and development of the disease focused on the possible role of the Epstein-Barr virus and of immune system deficiencies. Recent efforts involve postinfectious fatigue and blood pressure irregularities in CFS patients. Some agency efforts to develop diagnostic methods focus on the intensity of the symptoms and new measurement tools to evaluate CFS patients. NIH has also supported several projects with possible application to treatment, including modulating brain chemistry, developing individually tailored exercise programs, trials of pharmacologic agents, and studies of nonpharmacologic treatments. Given the limited understanding of the causes of CFS, work on NIAID's goal of furthering prevention has not been undertaken. Additional details about NIH's CFS research efforts and lists of the grants and projects funded by NIH are in appendix IV.

Some patient advocates have voiced concern that NIH has not funded specific kinds of CFS research, such as research on mycoplasma and its possible connection to CFS. However, we found no evidence that a grant proposal on mycoplasma had ever been submitted. Patient advocates have also criticized the types of CFS research that NIH has funded—in particular, psychiatric research. Some believe that NIH has disproportionately funded research of this type, but we found no such evidence. The National Institute for Mental Health's funding reported for CFS is artificially high because it includes funds for a large grant, of which only a small portion was related to CFS.

CDC and NIH Initiated Most Activities Requested by the Congress

Congressional interest in CFS research was first expressed in fiscal year 1988.[5] Since then, congressional report language, directed at both CDC and NIH, has indicated areas of research that the appropriations committees thought should be pursued. Both CDC and NIH have undertaken efforts in nearly all these areas. (A list of requested activities and their status is in app. V.)

---

[5]See H.R. Rep. No. 100-256, at 50 (1988); and S. Rep. No. 100-189, at 69 and 110 (1988).

Appropriations committees have requested in reports 33 distinct activities for CDC, including development and implementation of a surveillance network, continued tests related to specific suspected causes, and public information and training initiatives. CDC has initiated work on most of these. For the four areas where CDC did not initiate work, the agency reported that the work was inappropriate or not feasible for them to pursue.

NIH has also been largely responsive to congressional committee direction, appointing a CFS coordinator, ensuring appropriate representation to advisory committees and boards, and encouraging studies of risk factors and immunology. In report language, the appropriations committees have requested NIH work in 34 areas. All but five activities have been pursued; NIH considers some of those that have not been pursued infeasible.

CDC and NIH Initiated Most CFS-Related Activities in the Agencies' Own Program Plans and Responded to Recommendations of External Reviewers

CDC and NIH produced annual reports outlining their activities and plans for future work on CFS. For the most part, both agencies completed the work in those plans. To help the agencies stay focused on their goals, the agencies' review boards periodically examined the CFS program. At CDC, the CFS program has undergone a number of reviews. In 1991, CDC conducted an internal peer review of the CFS program by scientists from other CDC areas and programs. In 1993, there was an external peer review of the Viral Exanthems and Herpesvirus Branch, which included the CFS program. The CFS program underwent peer reviews in 1996 and 1999 as well as a review by CDC's Board of Scientific Counselors in 1999. At NIH, the National Advisory Allergy and Infectious Diseases Council discussed the CFS program in 1995, although components of the program were discussed at other meetings as well.

Scientists involved in the 1991 internal CDC peer review expressed concerns in four areas: (1) the limited sample size proposed for a case control study of CFS risk factors, (2) the statistical power of the case control study to detect real differences, (3) the lack of representativeness of the sample of patients referred by physicians in the surveillance study designed to estimate prevalence, and (4) the extensiveness of the factors to be evaluated in an exploratory study. The 1993 branch review suggested two specific additions to CDC's study of possible causes of CFS. They also recommended that CDC scientists contact those at NIH where a relevant study was under way. Agency officials reported that there was no official agency response to either review.

CDC's 1996 peer review, conducted by four scientists and two patient advocates, made 18 recommendations; for the most part, CDC has undertaken activities in response to these recommendations. CDC receive a consistent message from both the 1999 peer review and the review of it Board of Scientific Counselors that they should look for more opportunities to collaborate with other researchers, including possibly those at NIH. There were a number of other recommendations from thes recent reviews, and CDC officials have reported many activities planned address these recommendations. (See app. VI.)

NIAID's National Advisory Allergy and Infectious Diseases Council has al occasionally made recommendations about CFS research efforts. The council has advocated that the agency support specific studies suggested by findings from case demographics, encouraged continuing and expanding the CFS Cooperative Research Centers program, and determined at a fall 1995 CFS program review that NIAID should retain overall leadership of NIH's CFS efforts but that a multidisciplinary resear approach involving other institutes should also continue, where appropriate. A subcommittee of the council also recommended the agen develop work in a number of areas. NIH has conducted investigations in but two of these areas (studies of patients with shorter duration of illnes and issues related to pregnancy). (See app. VI.)

CDC's Funding Practices Have Impeded CFS Research in Contrast to NIH's

Researchers and patient advocates have expressed concerns about CDC and NIH's resources (funding and staffing) and funding mechanisms for CFS research, and their potential effects on the agencies' ability to plan a carry out research. Although CDC and NIH funds have increased over tin stabilizing in recent years, their funding data may not fully reflect their C expenditures due to each agency's process for tracking CFS funds. Staffi directly related to CFS has increased in recent years at CDC, but it has declined at NIH. We found that the processes and timing for distributing funds within CDC impeded CFS research and may reflect inadequate control on the part of the agency. Conversely, NIH has used a number of mechanisms to facilitate the support of CFS research, including progran announcements, the formation of a special review panel for CFS grant applications, and support of research centers.

CDC and NIH Resources for CFS Research Have Increased, but These Levels Have Been Flat Over the Past 4 Years

Since 1988, the congressional committee reports accompanying CDC's annual appropriation act have expressed an expectation that specific funds would be used for CFS research and other CFS projects. Although CDC has generally requested each year the same level of funding for CFS as was received the prior year, the committee reports suggest increasingly larger sums. The amount of funds suggested in these reports has increased from $407,000 in fiscal year 1988 to $6,497,000 in fiscal year 1999.[6] (See fig. 1.) However, since fiscal year 1995, the level of suggested funding increased only a total of $455,000. Moreover, the HHS Inspector General review found that over one-third of the funds ($8.8 million) in fiscal years 1995 through 1998 was spent on activities unrelated to CFS and another $4.1 million in indirect costs was not adequately documented to determine applicability to CFS. Regardless, CDC officials reported only one study—a survey of adolescents—that it did not initiate because of insufficient funds, and the agency has since determined that this study was not feasible for methodological reasons.

[6]For CDC, we refer only to funds budgeted for CFS research because the HHS Inspector General review of the CFS program at CDC found that CDC had been unable to clearly identify funds actually spent on CFS.

Figure 1: CDC Funding, Fiscal Years 1988 Through 1999

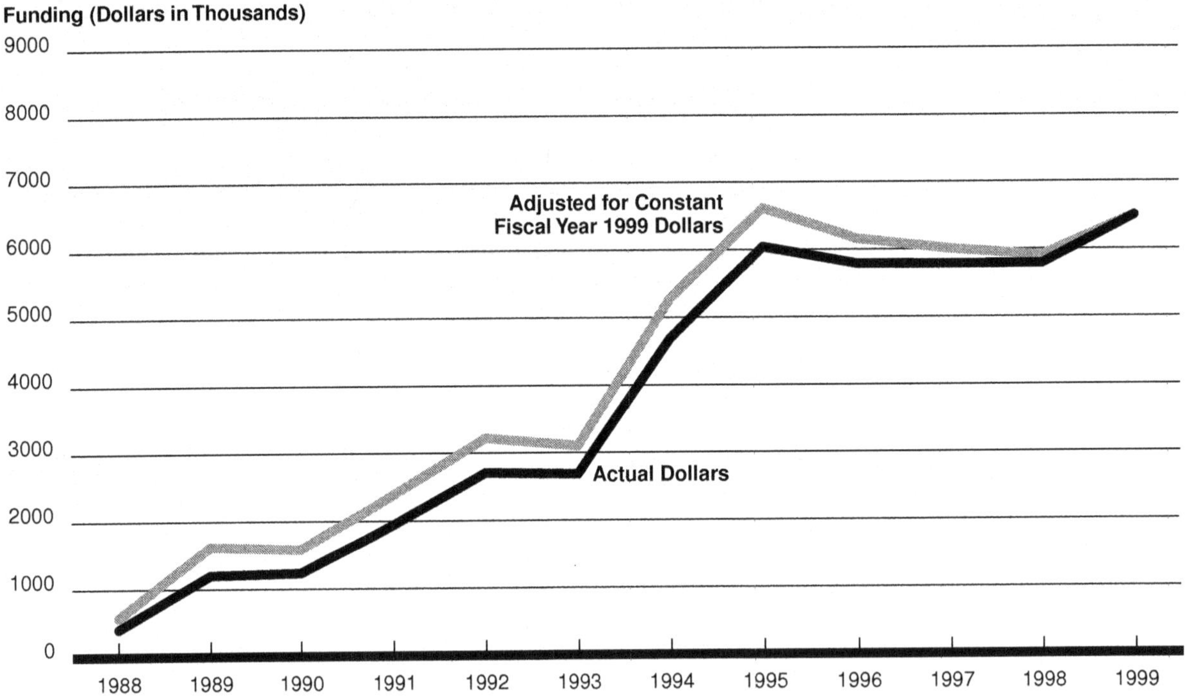

Funding (Dollars in Thousands)

CDC indicated that it has increased the number of staff working on CFS.[7] Prior to 1996, permanent staff working on CFS filled approximately 5 to 8 positions; since then, the number of positions has increased to 13 to 15. During these same periods, the staff has also changed from mostly permanent employees to mostly temporary employees. The temporary staff have typically been predoctoral or postdoctoral students or laboratory technicians.

---

[7]The staffing levels represent only those who work directly for CDC on CFS, although much of CDC's work on CFS is conducted extramurally, as is most of CDC work in general.

NIH expenditures for both intramural and extramural CFS projects increased from $782,000 in fiscal year 1987 to $6,892,000 in fiscal year 1999,[8] although these expenditures declined slightly over the last 4 years. (See fig. 2.) Further, while NIAID was the only institute to fund CFS research in the first 2 years (fiscal years 1987 through 1988), with minimal support from one other institute during the next 2 years, six institutes funded CFS research in fiscal year 1999. (See app. VII.) It is important to note that these figures may not accurately reflect expenditures for CFS. For the National Institute of Mental Health, expenditures are likely overestimated because projects are included even when only a small portion is relevant to CFS. For other institutes, expenditures may be underestimated for at least two reasons. First, if the institute or center has $250,000 or less in total funding for a disease, it is not required to report spending for that disease. Second, projects that are peripherally related to CFS may not have been included in NIH's funding figures.

---

[8]For NIH, we refer to expenditures—that is, funds that were spent on grants (extramural), projects (intramural), and cooperative agreements.

Figure 2: NIH Expenditures, Fiscal Years 1988 Through 1999

Expenditures (Dollars in Thousands)

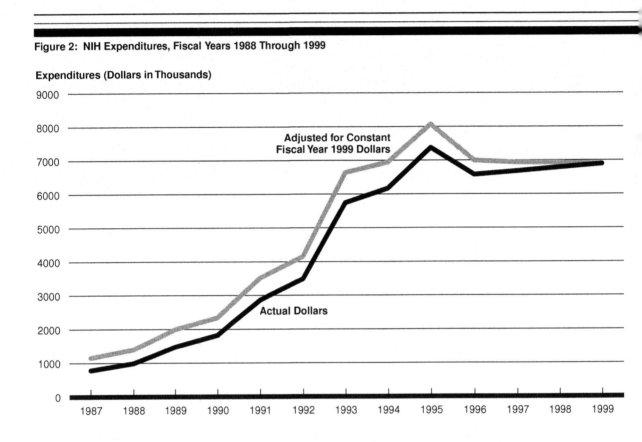

While NIH expenditures for CFS research have remained fairly stable over recent years, staffing levels at NIAID, the only institute for which we have data, have decreased.[9] Between 1988 and 1996, the number of full-time-equivalent intramural staff increased from 2.5 to 3.25 staff. Since 1997, however, the number of intramural full-time-equivalent staff at NIAID working on CFS decreased from 2 in 1997 to less than 1 in 1999. Most of the intramural staff working on CFS in NIAID specialized in either nursing or internal medicine. In addition to the intramural staff, NIAID has a program officer assigned to the Virology Branch (which is responsible for the extramural CFS work at NIAID). Over the years, the amount of time devoted by the program officer to CFS work versus other work has ranged from 20 to 60 percent.[10]

---

[9]The staffing levels represent only those scientists who work directly for NIH on CFS, although much of NIH's work on CFS is conducted extramurally, as is most of NIH work in general.

[10]According to agency officials, other staff—such as the division director, branch chief, committee management staff, and budget staff—also devote time to work on CFS at NIH.

CDC's Processes and Timing for Allocating Funds Has Impeded CFS Research

Concerns have been raised by patient advocates that funding practices at CDC may create barriers to planning and carrying out CFS research. Specific issues raised are that indirect costs charged to the CFS program are inordinately high and that the distribution of CFS funds is not timely. We found that, from fiscal years 1988 through 1999, an average of 45 percent of CFS funds at CDC covered indirect costs, with funds being taken from budgeted allocations at the agency (20 percent), center (13 percent), and division levels (12 percent) prior to being distributed to the Viral Exanthems and Herpesvirus Branch.[11] (See fig. 3.) These set percentages were taken from budgeted allocations without consideration for variability in use of services across different programs. CDC officials told us that the agency recently changed the way it calculates indirect costs at the agency level and that these changes were made in a manner consistent with recommendations in the Inspector General audit. In recent years (1998 through 1999), therefore, total indirect costs have been closer to 37.5 percent. Changes in methods for calculating indirect costs have not been implemented at the center level or below.[12] Regardless, CDC officials told us that other programs within the Division of Viral and Rickettsial Disease had similar proportions of funds deducted for indirect costs, so these percentages are not unique to CFS funds.

[11]Agency-level indirect costs pay for, among other things, all offices of program support, three facilities offices, design, construction, maintenance, a financial management office, human resources management, information resources management, utilities, a procureme[n]t and grants office, a management analysis and services office, and mail. Center-level indire[ct] costs are used to support the Office of the Director and the Scientific Resources Program. The Scientific Resources Program covers lab program services for all of the divisions and branches, including glassware, animal work, infrastructure, chemicals, and the making of reagents. The division portion of indirect costs has been used for, among other things, support of maintenance agreements on all equipment, telephones, hardware support of computers, and equipment for the Office of the Director (such as facsimiles and photocopiers).

[12]The agency continues to develop its procedures for calculating indirect costs and expec[ts] to have them finalized by fiscal year 2001. Each center is also developing procedures for calculating indirect costs, though these are not expected to be implemented until after th[e] agency procedures are implemented. Accordingly, the National Center for Infectious Diseases has requested an external review of its indirect cost methodology. Further, divisions will not begin similar work until after the centers have implemented their procedures.

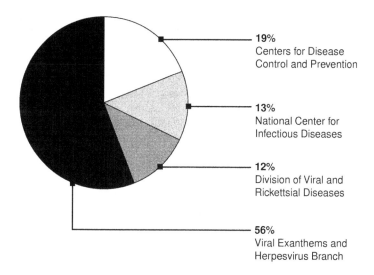

Figure 3: Proportion of CFS Funds Retained at Each Level of CDC, Fiscal Years 1998 Through 1999

19%
Centers for Disease
Control and Prevention

13%
National Center for
Infectious Diseases

12%
Division of Viral and
Rickettsial Diseases

56%
Viral Exanthems and
Herpesvirus Branch

The HHS Inspector General review of CFS found that the distribution of indirect costs agencywide may have been arbitrary and inconsistent, with some programs being significantly overcharged while other programs were charged far less than their fair share. The Inspector General also concluded that the various centers and divisions within CDC were able to arbitrarily determine the indirect costs for some or all of their programs, with no assurance that those charges would be reasonable and consistent. Further, the Inspector General found that the CFS program's indirect costs were largely undocumented and generally excessive in relation to those of other programs.

Although improvements in fund allocation have been made since 1998, the allocations of funds at CDC have typically been received late in the fiscal year—on average, more than 9 months into the fiscal year—which can adversely affect the ability to plan research programs. Moreover, funding allocations for the Viral Exanthems and Herpesvirus Branch have frequently not included explicit funding amounts for CFS. The National Center for Infectious Diseases has generally not received its final allocation from CDC until mid to late spring for the fiscal year that began the prior October.[13] The center then typically provided an allocation to the Division of Viral and Rickettsial Diseases 1 month later and the Division provided final allocation memorandums to the branches approximately 1 to 2 months after that. These timelines are typical across CDC. In fiscal years 1997 and 1998, the Viral Exanthems and Herpesvirus Branch received its allocation on July 7 or later—more than 9 months into the fiscal year.[14] Traditionally, the branch chiefs have been told to expect their budget to be about what it had been the previous year for planning purposes. However, uncertainties in funding levels have meant that the branch has planned or limited new work related to CFS each year.

The branch's allocation memorandums for fiscal years 1994, 1996, 1997, and 1998 did not include an allocation for CFS research.[15] That is, the allocation forms, received more than 9 months into the fiscal year, did not include any information about the level of funding available for the CFS program. For fiscal year 1998, final clarification about funds for CFS was not made until 9 days before the end of the fiscal year. Therefore, some CFS funds were not obligated by the end of the fiscal year and some program elements had to be suspended until the next fiscal year. However, in fiscal year 1999, the allocation memorandum to the branch chief clearly outlined the CFS funds available to the branch. This improvement may have been due to changes CDC had instituted in response to the 1999 HHS Inspector General review.

---

[13]Officials have said that CDC has recently improved this process. For example, agency officials reported that tentative ceilings were provided to the center within 30 calendar days of passage of its appropriations bill for fiscal year 1999 and within 17 calendar days for fiscal year 2000.

[14]Prior to fiscal year 1997, the Viral Exanthems and Herpesvirus Branch did not have an administrative officer, and budget allocations to the branch prior to that time did not indicate a date for the allocation.

[15]CDC was unable to provide allocation memorandums for any fiscal years prior to fiscal year 1994 or for fiscal year 1995.

Finally, the Inspector General review reported that CDC said it could not complete its adolescent study or hire a neuroendocrinologist because of a lack of available funds.[16] Nevertheless, the Inspector General found that, while program components were not implemented, more than $850,000 of fiscal year 1998 funds were never made available to the CFS program.

NIH Has Used a Number of Mechanisms to Facilitate Support of CFS Research

NIH develops extramural research on diseases, including CFS, primarily by creating program announcements for grant applications. The agency then relies on external researchers to decide what topics they want to pursue and funds meritorious applications up to the level of funds available. In addition to using program announcements to encourage extramural applications on CFS, NIH has created a special emphasis panel to review those applications, used selective payment, and established CFS cooperative research centers. NIH has also funded intramural investigations on CFS. Intramural research is determined by individual researchers and reviewed retrospectively. (See app. VIII for a more detailed description of these efforts.)

Since 1987, NIH has issued four program announcements to stimulate research on CFS. The first two program announcements were supported by NIAID only; the first, in 1987, focused on epidemiology; the second, in 1992, focused on exercise-induced fatigue and disease origin and development. In 1994, NIH issued its first joint program announcement, involving three institutes, which focused on studies of the causes, natural history, and origin and development of CFS. The most recent program announcement, issued in 1996, involves eight different units within NIH and supports studies on the effects of CFS on the body.

NIH established the CFS Special Emphasis Panel to review CFS grant applications. Agency officials reported that NIH did so to demonstrate the agency's commitment to CFS research because CFS is so little understood and so few applications for CFS were being received. The panels were designed to help facilitate the consideration and scoring of CFS grant applications that might otherwise not receive scores favorable enough to be funded if reviewed by the regular review panels. To date, a total of 30 extramural grants (or investigator-initiated research projects) reviewed by

---

[16]CDC has since initiated the hiring process of a neuroendocrinologist. We were told that the lengthy delay in hiring was due to a lack of an appropriate candidate, not a lack of funds. The adolescent study was later found not to be feasible for methodological reasons.

the panel have been funded. During the years that CFS grants have been funded (fiscal years 1988 through 1999), the funding rate for CFS was about 24 percent versus about 28 percent for all grants across the same institutes that fund CFS research. Officials at NIH have told us that, in their view, all meritorious CFS applications have been funded and that review by the special emphasis panel improves the chances that a CFS grant application will get a score that qualifies it for funding.

NIH has also used selective payment to facilitate the funding of CFS research. Selective payment is designed to provide funding to a small number of applications that are programmatically important but not rated favorably enough to receive funding otherwise. From 1992 through 1996, six CFS applications were funded through this process—all by NIAID; however, none have been funded through selective payment since 1996. NIH describes the selective payment process as designed to support applications that received scores just beyond the funding cut-off. However, it appears that NIAID made extra efforts to fund some CFS research because CFS applications funded through the selective payment process were ranked well beyond the funding cut-off.[17]

Since 1991, NIH has also issued three separate requests for applications for CFS cooperative research centers, supported with funds set aside for this purpose. The centers are designed to augment the existing grant program and to provide a sustained multidisciplinary approach to CFS research. The intent is to advance the field by bridging basic science and clinical research and facilitating confirmatory testing and follow-up of new hypotheses and observations. An NIH official told us that, each year, the agency plans to spend a certain amount on CFS. In fiscal year 1999, when NIH was unable to spend these funds on grants (because few were approved for funding), the agency chose to spend these funds on a third center, though only two had been initially planned for.

---

[17]The percentile rankings of all CFS applications funded under the selective payment program ranged from 53.7 to 75, well above what would be expected with just over 28 percent of the applications being funded overall. A high percentile ranking is assigned to applications with poor scores, and a low percentile ranking is assigned to those with good scores.

In addition to these sources of support for extramural work on CFS, NIH has also supported intramural work on CFS, most of it at NIAID. Intramural research activities have included studies of chronic viral infections and immunologic and endocrine systems. NIAID's intramural scientists have also been involved in a number of other collaborative activities.[18] Despite its varied efforts, the intramural program on CFS in NIAID is currently inactive. NIAID's primary CFS investigator has recently moved elsewhere in the agency, and we were told that no one else has yet indicated an interest in developing work in this area.

Limited Coordination Through Agency Efforts or CFSCC

Researchers and patient advocates have also expressed concerns about the extent to which the agencies obtain and use their input in developing research programs and about how CFSCC functions to coordinate agency efforts. While there has been interagency communication, coordination between CDC and NIH and involvement of patient advocates and external researchers have been limited. CFSCC has also had limited success in ensuring a coordinated research effort.

CDC and NIH Coordination and Involvement of Patient Advocates and External Researchers Limited

Although CDC and NIH officials reported frequent informal contacts, there are few formal mechanisms for interagency coordination. The director of the National Center for Infectious Diseases is an ex-officio member of NIAID's National Advisory Allergy and Infectious Diseases Council, and NIAID's Director of the Division of Microbiology and Infectious Diseases is an ex-officio member of the National Center for Infectious Diseases' Board of Scientific Counselors. Both advisory groups cover all areas of infectious disease—not just CFS. Officials at both CDC and NIH claimed that interagency coordination occurs through frequent and regular communication about CFS across the two agencies. We were also told that these communication efforts have been helpful and the quality of interagency communication has improved in recent years.

---

[18]NIAID intramural scientists collaborated with other NIH scientists on studies of the neuroendocrine system, seasonal variations in CFS patients, diagnosis and treatment of CFS, the measurement of fatigue, the characteristics of patients with CFS, memory function, and the relationships between CFS and induced episodes of illness and of fatigue. NIAID intramural scientists also collaborated with extramural researchers on a study of a therapy for neurally mediated hypotension. Neurally mediated hypotension is a disturbance in the autonomic nervous system's regulation of blood pressure and pulse, characterized by abnormally low blood pressure under certain circumstances.

However, there is little evidence of coordination between CDC and NIH on CFS research. While the missions of the two agencies are somewhat distinct, we identified no specific efforts to ensure that CFS research does not overlap or leave important gaps. For example, while CDC and NIH-funded researchers have shared preliminary manuscripts of their surveillance studies, both agencies have separately funded community-based surveillance research. We also identified no activities intended to build on the results of studies at the other agency, beyond generally reading the scientific literature.

Further, there have been no joint CFS research projects undertaken by CDC and NIH scientists. While CDC's peer review and Board of Scientific Counselors both recommended that there be more collaboration, projects of this type have not been initiated to date. CDC has indicated that it will share blood and serum samples with NIH intramural and extramural scientists when appropriate.

The agencies have used a number of mechanisms for soliciting the input of external researchers and patient advocates. CDC included CFS patient advocates on its two most recent CFS peer review teams, and NIH selected a CFS patient advocate to serve 4 years on its National Advisory Allergy and Infectious Diseases Council. Also, in 1998, patient advocates reviewed and commented on CDC's revised patient brochure, and in 1999, CDC convened a meeting of CFS patient advocacy group representatives to comment on various aspects of the CFS program. Further, external experts comprise NIH's CFS Special Emphasis Panel, reviewing grant applications

However, the agencies have not always sought the input of patient advocates and external researchers when there have been appropriate planning opportunities. For example, NIH officials responsible for what was initially intended to be a state-of-the-science meeting for CFSCC did not involve the patient advocate and scientific members of the committee in the planning process. This occurred despite the expressed interest of patient advocates and researchers who had a number of specific concerns about the selection of panelists.[19]

CFSCC Has Provided a Forum for Communication but Has Not Ensured a Coordinated Research Effort

While CFSCC has addressed a number of issues since it was chartered in 1996, it has made only limited progress in meeting its goals aimed at improving agencies' coordination of CFS research activities, programs, and education efforts.[20] Shortcomings in how the committee has functioned have hampered its progress; some of these shortcomings are beginning to be addressed.

Some CFSCC efforts have helped facilitate communication—particularly among representatives from FDA, the Health Resources and Services Administration, and the Social Security Administration—about CFS activities that are being carried out across HHS. For example, FDA used the CFS prevalence rates cited by CDC to determine whether a product would qualify for orphan drug designation.[21] To help address some research and educational needs, CFSCC identified gaps in knowledge and, in conjunction with their meetings, scheduled scientific discussion around

---

[19]Among the concerns patient advocates raised over the proposed list of participants are the following: (1) the list did not include any broad-based CFS experts, such as one of the past or present NIH CFS Cooperative Research Center directors; (2) the list did not include anyone who regularly saw CFS patients to draw on clinical experience; (3) two participants were included who are known for promoting psychiatric approaches to CFS and cognitive behavioral therapy research; and (4) an NIH scientist was asked to provide an overview of CFS research for the meeting, despite the scientist's no longer being actively involved in CFS research.

[20]CFSCC's five goals are (1) provide advice to the Secretary of HHS and others to ensure interagency coordination and communication regarding CFS research and other related issues, (2) develop complementary research programs that minimize overlap, (3) facilitate increased department and agency awareness of CFS research and educational needs, (4) identify collaborative and coordination opportunities in research and education, and (5) develop informed responses to constituency groups regarding agency efforts and progress.

[21]A product used to treat a rare disease affecting fewer than 200,000 Americans may be designated as an orphan drug and thereby qualifies the manufacturer for exclusive marketing for 7 years and tax incentives.

these topics, including adolescent CFS issues and physician education. CDC officials also reported that the agency provides funding to HHS' Health Resources and Services Administration and a patient advocacy organization to develop CFS educational materials. One CFSCC effort, currently under way, addresses patient advocates' concerns regarding the term "chronic fatigue syndrome," which they believe does not accurately reflect the nature of the disorder and stigmatizes individuals diagnosed with CFS. To address this issue, CFSCC has surveyed physicians, researchers, and patients and has formed a work group, with the involvement of the Assistant Surgeon General and the support of the Assistant Secretary of Health. CFSCC has also established a separate work group to review CFS' placement in the International Classification of Diseases, an international manual for classifying diseases. Committee consensus on this issue has not yet been reached.

Overall, however, CFSCC has made only limited progress in meeting the goals established by the Secretary to better coordinate CFS efforts. For example, CFSCC has not been a particularly useful forum for developing complementary research programs. At each of the committee's biannual meetings, representatives from each agency have described their recent CFS activities, but there has been little discussion about how to coordinate these activities. Moreover, according to agency officials, the meetings have had no effect on the direction of research at either CDC or NIH. However, agency officials stated that a change in the direction of research generally occurs as a result of relevant scientific or technical breakthroughs.

In addition, CFSCC has made only three recommendations to HHS' Secretary—and none have focused on interagency coordination. The first recommendation asked that HHS examine opportunities to combine existing data from various sources to better understand prevalence and epidemiology; the second asked the Secretary to help develop some clinically useful instruments that could be linked to other CFS information; and the third asked that the Secretary make more money available for CFS research to attract more researchers to the field. Regardless of the focus of these recommendations, the Secretary has not responded to any of them.

Patient advocates serving on CFSCC have voiced their dissatisfaction with the committee's ability to get information from the agencies. Specifically, they have been unable to obtain timely information from CDC and NIH necessary to carry out their advisory function and to be responsive to constituents. According to some of the patient advocate members, they repeatedly requested from each agency, over separate time periods, information on funding and research activities but did not receive the information in a timely fashion.

Based on our discussions with agency officials and CFSCC members, as well as a review of meeting transcripts, we found a number of shortcomings in the way the committee functions that may be limiting its effectiveness. Committee members cited a failure to

- discuss issues raised in agency reports and public testimony,
- develop recommendations for action, and
- develop continuity in the leadership of the committee because the cochair alternates between CDC and NIH every 2 years.

Much of the committee's meeting time is spent presenting reports from each agency on recent CFS activities. Minutes from the meetings show that, during CDC and NIH agency updates, the agencies' representatives rarely, if ever, questioned or discussed information in each other's updates. Meeting minutes also reflect no discussion of the issues raised during the public testimony portion of the meeting.

There are indications, however, that some of these shortcomings are beginning to be addressed. NIH changed its committee representative— who currently serves as cochair—from an official of NIAID to an official of NIH's Office of the Director. CFSCC members cited this as a positive development, viewing the centralized placement as more appropriate for facilitating cross-institute communication. In addition, CFSCC, during its February 2000 meeting, took steps to develop a new state-of-the-science meeting, establishing a planning committee chaired by a scientific member. This group will work between regular CFSCC meetings to facilitate more rapid progress on developing the state-of-the-science meeting; it should also provide greater committee control over the participants and agenda for this meeting. Finally, the cochair has invited all committee members to submit suggested format changes to make the meetings more productive. Some members of the committee believe that format changes will provide for greater discussion and progress and, therefore, coordination.

Conclusions

CDC has pursued avenues of research in a number of areas, in accordance with the agency's mission and congressional report language, including work on the case definition, surveillance, and risk factors for CFS. However, CDC's funding practices and redirection of CFS funds have delayed its research—evidenced by the agency's proposal to initiate an array of CFS projects, funded with the money it plans to restore. NIH has used a number of mechanisms to ensure that CFS research was funded. The development of program announcements, creation of the special emphasis panel, the use of selective payment, and support of cooperative research centers seem to demonstrate NIH's commitment to CFS research.

CFSCC has not been successful in meeting its goal: to ensure interagency coordination. While the committee has been useful in keeping both federal agencies and the public informed of current developments at the agencies and allowing the public an opportunity to raise issues that the committee might want to consider, it has yet to stimulate much discussion about how CDC and NIH could coordinate their programs. Recent actions within CFSCC to improve the structure of the meetings should help the committee move toward achieving its goals.

Agency Comments

We provided HHS the opportunity to comment on a draft of this report. HHS generally agreed with our findings and said that the report accurately conveyed the department's efforts on CFS. HHS specifically agreed that CFSCC could function more effectively as a coherent body with focus and direction. The department also provided technical comments, which we incorporated where appropriate. HHS' comments are reprinted in appendix IX.

As agreed with your office, unless you publicly announce the report's contents earlier, we plan no further distribution until 30 days from the date of this letter. We will then send copies to the Honorable Donna E. Shalala, Secretary of HHS; the Honorable Jeffrey P. Koplan, Director of CDC; the Honorable Ruth Kirschstein, Acting Director of NIH; and others who are interested. If you have any questions or would like additional information, please call me at (202) 512-7114. Marcia Crosse, Carolyn Feis, and Donald Keller made major contributions to this report.

Sincerely yours,

Janet Heinrich
Associate Director, Health Financing and
 Public Health Issues

Background on Chronic Fatigue Syndrome

CFS Case Definition

Under the first U.S. CFS case definition, developed in 1988, a case had to fulfill 2 major criteria and at least 8 of the 11 symptom criteria or at least 6 of those symptom criteria and 2 of 3 physical criteria. One major criterion was that there be a "new onset of persistent or relapsing, debilitating fatigue or easy fatigability in a person who has no previous history of similar symptoms, that does not resolve with bed rest, and that is severe enough to produce or impair average daily activity below 50 percent of the patient's premorbid activity level, for a period of at least 6 months."[1] The other major criterion was that other clinical conditions capable of causing similar symptoms had to be absent upon a thorough clinical evaluation. The list of the other conditions included over a dozen broad categories of disease, such as malignancy, autoimmune disease, chronic psychiatric disease, and chronic cardiac disease. The symptom criteria, which also had to persist or recur over at least 6 months, were specifically defined levels and/or kinds of fever, sore throat, sore lymph nodes, muscle weakness, muscle discomfort, prolonged fatigue induced by exercise, headaches, joint pain, neuropsychologic complaints, sleep disturbance, and development of the symptom complex over a period of a few hours to a few days (not a symptom but a criterion treated like the symptom criteria for purposes of the case definition). The physical criteria were specific, documented levels of fever, sore throat, and palpable or tender lymph nodes.

This first CFS case definition caused many difficulties for researchers. For example, the definition did not appear to distinguish CFS from other types of unexplained fatigue or define a distinct group of cases. As a result, another CDC consensus panel revised the U.S. definition of CFS in 1994. According to this second definition, in order to receive a diagnosis of CFS, a patient case must satisfy two criteria: (1) severe chronic fatigue of 6 months or longer duration with other known medical conditions excluded by clinical diagnosis and (2) four or more of the following symptoms concurrently: substantial impairment in short-term memory or concentration; sore throat; tender lymph nodes; muscle pain; pain in multiple joints without swelling or redness; headaches of a new type, pattern, or severity; unrefreshing sleep; and postexertional malaise lasting more than 24 hours. The symptoms must have persisted or recurred during 6 or more consecutive months of illness and must not have predated the fatigue. There are currently no laboratory tests to diagnose CFS, and there

---

[1] G. P. Holmes and others, "Chronic Fatigue Syndrome: A Working Case Definition," *Annals of Internal Medicine*, Vol. 108 (1988), pp. 387-9.

are a number of other illnesses that have a spectrum of symptoms similar to CFS, such as fibromyalgia, myalgic encephalomyelitis, neurasthenia, multiple chemical sensitivities, and chronic mononucleosis. Further, there are a large number of other illnesses that can result in fatigue, the diagnosis of which would preclude a diagnosis of CFS, such as major depressive disorders, hypothyroidism, cancer, and others.

Estimates of CFS Prevalence

CFS does not appear to be as rare as was originally suggested. Table 1 shows that estimates of CFS prevalence have increased over time as new data have been obtained and the definition of CFS has been modified. The estimates described here are based on data from samples of geographically defined populations, as opposed to individual clinics or health groups, and are based on patients who have been clinically evaluated relative to the case definition—not on patients' self-identification of chronic fatigue. Early CDC estimates—derived from data provided by physicians in four cities (Atlanta, Georgia; Wichita, Kansas; Grand Rapids, Michigan; and Reno, Nevada) who referred patients with CFS—were minimum prevalence rates, over a 2-year period, ranging across cities from 2.0 to 7.3 per 100,000.[2] A subsequent report based on more data from the same sources yielded age-, sex-, and race-adjusted rates over a 4-year period, ranging across cities from 4.0 to 8.7 per 100,000.[3] A more recent CDC study that looked only at persons aged 18 to 69 in Wichita used a more valid community sampling procedure to find cases, and had additional refinements of study design and data analysis yielded an adjusted prevalence rate for 1997 of 183 per 100,000.[4]

[2]W. J. Gunn and others, "Epidemiology of Chronic Fatigue Syndrome: The Centers for Disease Control Study," *Ciba Foundation Symposium*, Vol. 173 (1993), pp. 83-101.

[3]M. Reyes and others, "Surveillance for Chronic Fatigue Syndrome—Four U.S. Cities, September 1989 Through August 1993," *Morbidity and Mortality Weekly Report*, Vol. 46 (SS-2) (Feb. 21, 1997), p. 1-13.

[4]M. Reyes and others, "Random-Digit-Dialing Survey of Fatiguing Illness in Sedgwick County, Kansas (Wichita)." Paper presented at the American Association for Chronic Fatigue Syndrome International Research Conference (Boston, Mass., Oct. 10, 1998).

When CDC reanalyzed the data from Wichita and included for the first tim complete data from certain participants whose data were initially incomplete, the adjusted prevalence rate was reported to be 238 per 100,000.[5] The research team that conducted a population-based study in Chicago, funded by NIH, reported an overall estimated prevalence rate o 422 per 100,000.[6] The estimated rate for women was reported to be even higher: 522 per 100,000.

Table 1: U.S. Studies of CFS Prevalence Based on Clinical Evaluation of Samples of Local Populations

Study	Method[a]	Rates (per 100,000)	Estimated number of peo with CFS in U.S. popula
Gunn and others (1993), four cities	2-year prevalence	2.0-7.3	4,000-14,
Reyes and others (1997), four cities	4-year prevalence, adjusted	4.0-8.7	8,000-17,
Reyes and others (1998), Wichita	Prevalence, adjusted	183	363,
Reeves (1999), Wichita	Prevalence, adjusted	238	471,
Jason and others (1999), Chicago	Prevalence	422	836,

[a]Adjusted for age, sex, and race, where indicated.

Research on Possible Causes of CFS

There have been many hypotheses about the cause or causes of CFS. On possibility is that an infectious agent, such as the Epstein-Barr virus, is t cause of CFS, but a systematic association between CFS and Epstein-Ba virus has not been found.[7] Similarly, many known human infectious ager including other viruses and nonviral pathogens have been studied as possible causes of CFS.[8] So far, none of the infectious agents studied hav been found to be significantly associated with CFS. It is possible, howev

---

[5]W. Reeves at meeting of Chronic Fatigue Syndrome Coordinating Committee (Washingt D.C., Apr. 22, 1999).

[6]L. A. Jason and others, "A Community-Based Study of Chronic Fatigue Syndrome," *Archives of Internal Medicine*, Vol. 159 (1999), pp. 2129-37.

[7]Epstein-Barr virus has been implicated in a number of medical conditions, including mononucleosis, and the similarity of CFS to chronic mononucleosis led to the hypothes that CFS was due to chronic Epstein-Barr infection.

[8]Causes that have been studied include, for example, human retroviruses, human herpesvirus 6, enteroviruses, rubella, Borna disease viruses, Candida albicans, and mycoplasma.

that an unknown or rarely studied infectious agent is the cause, or that CFS has many different infectious causes, each one of which is responsible for only a subset of CFS cases. Further, viral infection is one of many conditions proposed, along with other transient traumatic conditions, stress, and toxins, to trigger, but not necessarily sustain, the development of CFS.

Another vigorously pursued possibility is that CFS is caused by an immunologic dysfunction, such as lower numbers of the immune system components called "natural killer cells" or an inappropriate production of the natural body chemicals known as "cytokines." Several immune system abnormalities and histories of allergies have been observed in CFS patients, but none of them consistently. Moreover, CFS patients have not been shown to have the tissue damage found in autoimmune diseases, such as rheumatoid arthritis. Nor do they typically manifest the susceptibility to opportunistic infections or increased cancer risk so often found in persons with deficient or suppressed immune systems, such as AIDS patients. It is also possible that if there are immune system abnormalities in patients with CFS, the abnormalities are themselves caused by infectious agents, other specific kinds of exposure, or stress. There has been no empirical support for any of these specific hypotheses involving an immunologic cause, but it is possible that immunologic dysfunction plays a role, perhaps a complex one, in the development of some or all cases of CFS.

The infectious and immunologic etiological hypotheses are not the only ones that have been explored for CFS. Two hypotheses related to the nervous system have also generated considerable research. First, it has been observed that CFS patients secrete lower than normal levels of the hormone cortisol in response to physical or emotional stress. The hypothesis that has resulted from this observation is that the neuroendocrine system, which is involved in these secretions via the hypothalamus and pituitary gland of the brain (the hypothalamic-pituitary-adrenal axis), has an important role in CFS. However, the difference in cortisol levels between patients and healthy control subjects does not appear great enough to account for CFS. Second, it has been hypothesized that disturbances in the autonomic nervous system's regulation of blood pressure and pulse, characterized by abnormally low blood pressure under certain circumstances, play an important role in CFS. This condition is known as neurally mediated hypotension. As in the cases of the infectious and immune system hypotheses, conclusive support for the involvement of either the hypothalamic-pituitary-adrenal axis or neurally mediated hypotension in all or most cases of CFS has not been found.

Accounting Issues at CDC

In 1998, a CDC employee alleged that CDC had diverted CFS funds to other programs and had provided erroneous information to the Congress regarding the scope and costs of CFS research. At the request of CDC, HHS Inspector General conducted an audit to determine whether costs charged to the CFS program from fiscal years 1995 through 1998 were actually incurred for that program in accordance with applicable laws, regulations and accounting standards. CDC is not legally prohibited from spending funds budgeted for CFS on other programs because the Congress did not make specific line item appropriations to that program. However, it is clear from Senate, House, and Conference report language that CDC was expected to spend the amount budgeted for CFS only on CFS.

HHS' Inspector General found that a significant portion of CFS funds were spent on other programs and activities and that CDC failed to adequately document the relevance of other costs charged to CFS. The Inspector General accepted 43 percent of the expenditures as actually incurred for program purposes, could not accept 39 percent because they were incurred for non-CFS-related activities, and could not determine the applicability of 18 percent of indirect costs because of insufficient documentation. The Inspector General found that the questionable charges resulted from deficiencies in CDC's internal control system for handling direct and indirect costs. The Inspector General also found that, as a result, CDC officials provided inaccurate information to the Congress.

The Inspector General further determined that CDC did not have adequate controls to ensure that direct costs charged at the program activity level are based on the actual efforts of involved personnel. As a result, the Director of the Division of Viral and Rickettsial Diseases was able to transfer to CFS unrelated costs without appropriate analysis, documentation, or justification. Similarly, the Inspector General determined that CDC had inadequate controls to ensure that indirect cost from all organizational levels were properly identified and consistently allocated.

In response to the Inspector General report, CDC will restore $12.9 million in funding to the CFS program over 4 years. This is identical to the sum of funds the Inspector General did not accept as related to CFS ($8.8 million and was questionable ($4.1 million). CDC also promised a number of corrections:

- A public apology to the Congress from the Director of CDC and other senior staff.

- Probationary status for the Division of Viral and Rickettsial Diseases with regard to budget execution until January 2001.
- Separate apportionment of CFS funds from the Office of Management and Budget with the accompanying requirement that an operating plan be submitted to the Congress. Accordingly, quarterly reports will be submitted to the Congress regarding the budgetary execution of this plan.
- Mandatory training for all CDC managers and staff responsible for budget and accounting functions to ensure complete knowledge of statutory and regulatory requirements for the use of federal funds.
- Establishment of an internal review capacity to conduct regular assessments of CDC's fiscal policies, procedures, practices, and controls.
- Development and implementation of a new system for allocation of CDC-wide indirect program support costs.
- Reinvigoration of CDC's efforts to better understand CFS by establishing a long-term research and program agenda with in-depth advice from the research and advocacy communities.

A subsequent accounting analysis of fiscal year 1999 CFS expenditures, conducted by PricewaterhouseCoopers, an independent auditing firm, found that 99.2 percent of the fiscal year 1999 funds reported by CDC as CFS obligations were in fact related to CFS program activities. They also found that CDC adequately addressed the concerns raised by the Inspector General report for the CFS program for fiscal year 1999.

In February 2000, there were public reports that similar accounting difficulties extended beyond the CFS program. Specifically, it had been reported that CDC also spent funds intended for the study of hantavirus on other diseases. The PricewaterhouseCoopers analysis of fiscal year 1999 CFS expenditures also recommended that the CDC strongly consider conducting an accounting analysis of the obligations reported for the hantavirus program for fiscal years 1995 through 1998. In response to these concerns, CDC made management changes at the level of the Director of the Division of Viral and Rickettsial Diseases, responsible for both the CFS and hantavirus programs. In addition, the Secretary of HHS, in consultation with the Director of CDC, told the Congress that a number of additional corrective actions were under way:

- HHS' Chief Financial Officer will take such actions as necessary to certify all financial obligations made by the National Center for Infectious Diseases for the remainder of fiscal year 2000.

- HHS' Chief Financial Officer will work with the Director of CDC to ensure that all senior decisionmakers in the National Center for Infectious Diseases receive certified budget execution training.
- CDC is commissioning an external review of the agency's fiscal management practices. The review is to be completed by September 2000. The results of the analysis will be communicated to the Congress as soon as the review is complete.
- CDC program managers will conduct a top-to-bottom examination of CDC's programs and projects to make sure there are no other areas of concern. During the 90-day period, CDC managers will be able to fully and openly identify any area for which there may be a discrepancy between actual expenditures and the information provided to the Congress. CDC will share these findings with the Congress.
- CDC has commissioned PricewaterhouseCoopers to thoroughly examine the hantavirus expenditures. The results will be communicated to the Chair of the Senate Subcommittee on Labor, Health and Human Services, Education and Related Agencies, Committee on Appropriations, immediately upon completion. When the audit is complete, CDC will expand the effort to the entire National Center for Infectious Diseases.

CDC Research Efforts and Publications

CDC, with others, developed the first case definition of CFS in 1988 and the second definition in 1994. These case definitions reflect clinical judgment gathered from experience with patients sick enough and with sufficient resources to seek medical care. Neither of the case definitions has been derived from quantitative clinical data, such as lab results, because there are no known markers for infection and, consequently, no laboratory tests available. CDC recently met to consider the need for another revision of the case definition, which may change the number of people who could be diagnosed with CFS, as occurred when the definition was broadened in 1994 and more people met the revised definition's criteria. While higher prevalence estimates can be helpful to research by potentially attracting more funding and more research interest, it can also mask possible research findings—that is, if the population now defined as having CFS is heterogeneous, it may be more difficult to identify causes.

CDC has conducted a number of surveillance studies to determine the prevalence of CFS, including a four-city study using physician referrals to identify possible CFS patients. CDC was criticized for using physician referrals because patient frustration over physicians who do not understand CFS or over insurance difficulties may result in CFS patients not being in the health care system. A CDC official offered many justifications for this approach, including its past use for other diseases, the participation of most primary care physicians in the areas studied, and the ability to gather data annually. Further, we were told that the study was the most rigorous that could be performed with the funds that were available to the agency at that time and that the prevalence estimates could be used to estimate the burden of CFS on the health care system.

CDC shifted from this passive surveillance approach to a more active approach when it conducted a pilot study of randomly selected individuals in San Francisco, California. Based on this pilot, the agency began a large-scale study in Wichita, Kansas. Here, almost 7,000 subjects are being followed annually for 3 years. However, because most participants in the Wichita sample are white, the sample may not be adequate for studying the prevalence of CFS in racial and ethnic minorities. Regardless, a CDC official told us that Wichita was chosen because it is representative of the United States with respect to its racial and ethnic makeup. Further, the population of Wichita is relatively stable, allowing for the long-term follow-up called for by the study. CDC uses interview and clinical data from participants in these studies to describe the epidemiology of fatiguing illnesses. For example, blood and other specimens are collected from those enrolled in the clinical evaluation component of the study to be used in laboratory studies to identify risk factors and diagnostic markers. CDC is also taking additional steps to estimate prevalence. The agency is currently developing a national study to estimate sex-, age-, race/ethnic-, and socioeconomic-specific prevalence of CFS. Finally, late in fiscal year 2000 CDC plans to begin developing a national CFS patient registry where patients will be followed yearly.

To date, CDC studies of risk factors and diagnostic markers associated with CFS have not identified consistently strong and significant associations between CFS and exposure to infectious agents or abnormalities in immune function.[1] In efforts to understand the physiological basis of CFS, CDC established a group to examine genetic issues in CFS and further identify risk factors and diagnostic markers. CDC also has investigated suspected clusters of CFS in seven different locations but was unable to confirm any clusters in these areas.

CDC has presented only limited data on the natural course of the disease, relying on data collected from their longitudinal surveillance studies, which have taken years to conduct. Further, CDC has acknowledged the limitations in the data it has published from its four-city physician-based study. CDC has noted that the study was limited because most patients had been ill for many years and no clinical data were gathered to further support the symptoms described by patients, observed by providers, or both. To supplement this work, CDC continues to gather data from the Wichita area that include baseline and annual follow-ups for 3 years.

CDC has undertaken a variety of efforts to educate practitioners, professionals, and the public. Scientists from CDC have published numerous articles describing their work, and a CDC official reported that peer-reviewed publications, listed in figure 4, were the cornerstone of the education efforts for physicians.

---

[1]For example, CDC has looked at the association of CFS with chronic enteroviral infection, associated viral infections and immunological abnormalities; viruses like human T-cell lymphotropic virus type II; retroviruses; Borna disease virus; physical, behavioral, and psychological risk factors; strain differences in common viral infections; and neuroendocrine function. Laboratory work has involved immune function assays, including lymphocyte markers, cytokines, natural killer cell dysfunction, serum Ig levels, complement levels, and immune complexes. CDC also cultured specimens in attempts to isolate herpesvirus 6 and 7.

Figure 4: CDC Publications

CDC PUBLICATIONS
ON CHRONIC FATIGUE SYNDROME
1987-1999

1. Case Definition

Holmes GP, et al. Chronic fatigue syndrome: a working case definition. Ann Intern Med 1988;108:3879.

Holmes GP. Defining the chronic fatigue syndrome. Rev Infect Dis 1991;13(suppl 1):S53-5.

Fukuda K. The chronic fatigue syndrome: a comprehensive approach to its definition and study. Ann Intern Med 1994: 121:953-9.

Fukuda K. Development of the 1994 chronic fatigue syndrome case definition and clinical evaluation guidelines. In: Yehuda S, Mostofsky D. Chronic fatigue syndrome. New York: Plenum Press, 1997:29-50.

2. Etiology

Holmes GP. The chronic fatigue syndrome. In Schlossberg D. Infectious mononucleosis, 2nd ed. New York: Springer-Verlag. 1989:172-93.

ReevesWC, Pellett PE, Gary HE. The CFS controversy [letter]. Ann Intern Med 1992;117:343-4.

Khan AS, et al. Assessment of a retrovirus sequence and other possible risk factors for the chronic fatigue syndrome. Ann Intern Med 1993;118:241-5.

Folks TM, et al. Investigation of retroviral involvement in chronic fatigue syndrome. In chronic fatigue syndrome. Wiley. Chichester, 1993; 160-75.

CDC. Inability of retroviral tests to identify persons with CFS. MMWR 1993;42:183,9,90.

Heneine W, Folks TM. Retroviruses and chronic fatigue syndrome. In: Chronic fatigue syndrome. New York: Marcel Dekker, 1994:199-206.

Black JB Human herpes virus 7 – a new challenge. Virus Life 1994;11:14-16.

1

Mawle AC, Reyes M, Schmid DS. Is chronic fatigue syndrome an infectious disease? Infect Agents Disease 1994;2:333-41.

Heneine W, et al. Lack of evidence for infection with known human and animal retroviruses in patients with CFS. Clin Infect Dis 1994;18(S-1):S121-5.

Stewart JA, Patton JL. Human herpesvirus 6 and other human herpesviruses. In: Murray PR et al. Manual of clinical microbiology. 6th ed. Washington DC: ASM 1995:911-7.

Dobbins JG, et al. Physical, behavioral, and psychological risk factors for CFS: a central role for stress? J Chronic Fat Syndr 1995;1:43-58.

Mawle AC, Nisenbaum R, Dobbins JG, Gary HE, Stewart JA, Reyes M, Steele L, Schmid DS, Reeves WC. Seroepidemiology of chronic fatigue syndrome: a case-control study. Clin Infect Dis 1995;21:1386-9.

Mawle AC, Nisenbaum R, Dobbins JG, Gary HE, Stewart JA, Reyes M, Steele L, Schmid DS, Reeves WC. Immune responses associated with chronic fatigue syndrome: a case-control study. J Infect Dis 1996;175:136-41.

Pellett, PE, Black JB. Human herpesvirus 6. In Fields *Virology* (Fields, BN, DM Knipe, and PM Howley, eds), 3rd edition, Raven Press, NY 1996; pp. 2548-2608.

Reyes M, Dobbins JG, Mawle AC, Steele L, Gary HE, Malani H, Schmid S, Fukuda K, Stewart J, Nisenbaum R, Reeves WC. Risk factors for CFS: a case control study. J Chron Fatigue Synd 1996;2:17-33.

Black, JB, TF Schwarz, JL Patton, K Kite-Powell, PE Pellett, S Wiersbitzky, R Bruns, C Muller, G Jager, JA Stewart. Evaluation of Immunoassays for detection of antibodies to human herpesvirus 7. Clin Diag Lab Immunol 3:79-83, 1996.

Braun DK, Dominguez G, Pellett PE. Human herpesvirus 6. Clin Micro Rev 1997;10:521-567.

Nisenbaum R, Reyes, M, Mawle AC, Reeves WC. Factor analysis of unexplained severe fatigue and interrelated symptoms: overlap with criteria for chronic fatigue syndrome. Am J Epidemiol 1998;148:72-7.

Stewart JA, Lennette, E, Patton JL. Human herpesvirus 6, 7, and 8 and other herpesviruses. In: Murray PR, Baron EJ, Pfaller MA, Tenover FC, Yolken RH, eds.

2

Manual clinical microbiology, 7th ed. Washington DC: American Society for Microbiology, 1998.

Meng Y-X, Pellett PE. Recently discovered herpesviruses: human herpesviruses 6, 7, and 8. In Ahmed R, Chen I, eds., Persistent viral infections, John Wiley and Sons. 1999.

3. Surveillance

Gunn WJ, et al. Epidemiology of chronic fatigue syndrome: the Centers for Disease Control study. In Chronic fatigue syndrome. Wiley, Chichester;1993:83-101.

Reyes M, Gary HE, Dobbins JG, Steele L, Randall B, Fukuda K, Holmes GP, Connell DG, Mawle A, Schmid DS, Stewart JA, Schonberger LB, Gunn WJ, Reeves WC. Surveillance for chronic fatigue syndreome – four U.S. cities September 1989 through August 1993. MMWR Surveill Summ 1997;46:2-13.

Steele L, Dobbins JG, Fukuda K, Reyes M, Randall B, Koppelman M, Reeves WC. The epidemiology of chronic fatigue in San Francisco. Am J Med 1998;105(3A):83S-90S.

4. Cluster Investigations

Holmes GP. A cluster of patients with a chronic mononucleosis-like syndrome. JAMA 1987;257:2297-302.

CDC. Unexplained illness among Persian Gulf War veterans in an Air National Guard unit: preliminary report – August 1990-March 1995. MMWR 1995;44:443-7.

Fukuda K, Dobbins JG, Wilson LJ, Dunn RA, Wilcox K, Smallwood D. An epidemiologic study of fatigue with relevance for the chronic fatigue syndrome. J Psychiatric Res 1997;31:19-29.

Shefer A, Dobbins JG, Fukuda K, Steele L, Koo D, Nisenbaum R, Rutherford GW. Fatiguing illness among employees in three large state office buildings, California 1993: was there an outbreak? J Psychiatric Res 1997;31:31-43.

Fukuda K, Nisenbaum R, Stewart G, Thompson WW, Robin L, Washko RM, Noah DL, Barrett DH, Randall B, Herwaldt BL, Mawle AC, Reeves WC. A chronic multisymptom illness affecting Air Force veterans of the Persian Gulf War. JAMA 1998;280:981-8.

3

5.   Adolescents

Dobbins JG, Randall B, Reyes M, Steele L, Livens EA, Reeves WC. Prevalence of chronic fatiguing illness among adolescents in the United States. J Chronic Fatigue Syndrome 1997;3:15-28.

6.   Clinical Course/Patient Management

Gantz NM, Holmes GP. Treatment of patients with chronic fatigue syndrome. Drugs 1989; 38:855-62.

Fukuda K, Gantz NM. Management stategies for chronic fatigue syndrome. Federal Practioner July 1995.

Reyes M, Dobbins JG, Nisenbaum R, Subedar NS, Randall B, Reeves WC. Chronic fatigue syndrome progression and self-defined recovery: evidence from the CDC Surveillance System. J Chronic Fatigue Syndrome 1999;5(1): 17-27.

7.   Molecular Epidemiology

Dimulescu I, Unger ER, Lee DR, Vernon SD. Characterization of RNA in cytologic samples preserved in a methanol based collection medium. Molecular Diagnosis 3:1-7, 1998.

Rajeevan MS, Dimulescu IM, Unger ER, Vernon SD. Chemiluminescent analysis of gene expression on high density filter arrays. J Histochemistry Cytochemistry 1999; 47:337-42.

8.   Health Education

CDC. The facts about chronic fatigue syndrome (brochure), Atlanta: Centers for Disease Control and Prevention, 1998.

4

Source: CDC.

In addition, CDC has established a web site devoted to CFS containing hundreds of pages of materials, has maintained a toll-free hot line, and ha developed a booklet about CFS, which has been revised twice. Further,

CDC has presented information at conferences for CFS patient support groups and other professional associations. CDC acknowledges that some physicians might not recognize CFS as a distinct illness. As a result, CDC plans to add a medical education specialist to its staff in fiscal year 2000 to develop a more rounded and aggressive medical education program aimed at health care providers, public health officials at the state and local levels, health maintenance organizations, and insurance providers.

CDC has been criticized for delays in releasing the findings of its studies and for the breadth of its research. CDC sometimes does not release findings from its studies until they are published in a professional journal. The publication process can take months or years, meaning that the latest information may not always be immediately available. However, CDC officials told us they use professional journals to communicate with the medical community—the generally accepted way to disseminate results from scientific studies. Further, the peer review that is often required prior to publication can serve to validate its findings. Second, some scientists feel that certain areas of research have not been adequately or appropriately pursued. For example, some were concerned that valuable data would be lost when CDC proposed selecting new patients for future work, rather than continuing to work with those patients who had been part of the Wichita study for 3 years. In addition, it has been suggested that CDC's efforts to replicate findings on certain types of viruses did not use the same methodology as in the original study and, therefore, CDC's failure to replicate the findings was based on a flawed design. CDC officials stated that the agency plans to continue working with patients identified during the Wichita study as part of future clinical and laboratory investigations. CDC officials also reported that the agency uses the most current and appropriate methods to identify infectious agents. According to agency officials, where these differ from those in an original study, it is because CDC has determined new or better methods exist.

NIH Research Efforts and Grants

NIH Research Efforts

The National Institute of Allergy and Infectious Diseases (NIAID) has pursued the goal of studying the causes of CFS, including the search for risk factors and diagnostic markers, more extensively than any of its other CFS-related goals. A number of the other institutes have supported collaborative or complementary work on causes. NIH has funded investigations of immunologic, neuropsychologic, neuroendocrinologic, brain wave, and infectious aspects of CFS, any of which might have implications for understanding causes.[1] Studies of subtypes of CFS have also been conducted.

Although CDC has taken the lead in efforts to estimate the prevalence of CFS, NIAID has also supported a number of attempts to establish the magnitude of the problem. In the early 1990s, it funded research in Seattle and Boston estimating CFS prevalence in primary care settings. In 1995, began funding a large epidemiological project in Chicago to study the socioeconomic and ethnic variability of CFS. This project has generated population-based prevalence estimates for the overall population and for racial and other subgroups, such as women.

NIH has supported research on the origins and development of CFS. Early work focused on the possible role of Epstein-Barr virus in CFS and on certain immune system deficiencies thought to occur in CFS. The two most recent efforts involve a model of postinfectious fatigue, which may provide insight into what happens when a person contracts CFS after an infection and blood pressure irregularities in CFS patients.

NIH has supported some efforts to develop clinically useful diagnostic methods. The early work in this area involved distinguishing chronic, active Epstein-Barr infection from diagnosed CFS. More recently, NIH has supported a study of the effective diagnosis of chronic fatigue and its intensity and a study of the feasibility of using specific measurement tools to evaluate CFS patients.

---

[1]NIH funded a number of studies comparing CFS patients and healthy controls with respect to potential laboratory markers and risk factors, including sleep patterns and various neurologic, virologic, and immunologic features. Some additional etiological hypotheses that were tested include those implicating orthostatic intolerance, other aspects of cardiac regulation, hypothalamic dysfunction, autoantibody responses, allergies, and the dysregulation of specific antiviral pathways.

NIH has supported several projects with possible application to treatment. These include modulating brain chemistry and developing individually tailored exercise programs. Other efforts have included trials of pharmacologic agents and studies of nonpharmacologic treatments.

Work on NIAID's goal of furthering prevention would be premature given the limited understanding of the causes of CFS, and NIH has not supported efforts in this direction. However, NIH has supported a number of relevant efforts not explicitly linked to any of its stated goals, such as activities contributing to the education of researchers—chiefly workshops and other kinds of meetings—and to a lesser extent, the education of practitioners and the public, chiefly pamphlets about CFS.

Researchers and patient advocates have criticized NIH's efforts on CFS research. Some have suggested that studies in certain areas have not been adequately investigated. In at least one situation, it has been speculated that NIH investigators did not pursue a particular finding because the finding was possibly contrary to what was expected. We were also told that prominent researchers have been turned down for funding, discouraging them from staying in the field. Some patient advocates have argued that NIH is increasingly funding research on mental health and its relation to CFS, but the evidence does not support this assertion. While it appears that the National Institute of Mental Health has spent more funds on CFS research than any institute other than NIAID, this is an artifact of the data management system at NIH. The majority of these funds were allocated to a study encompassing a range of work, only a small portion of which was related to CFS. In fact, National Institute of Mental Health officials told us that they do not consider CFS to be a mental disorder and that CFS is not listed in the diagnostic manual used in psychiatry and psychology. They further do not consider themselves to have an ongoing program on CFS; rather they occasionally study CFS because of interest in certain relevant hypotheses. Nevertheless, these concerns are indicative of the doubt and mistrust that both researchers and patient advocates expressed.

NIH-Funded Grants and Projects Related to CFS

Due to concerns we heard about inconsistencies between CFS grants listed in NIH reports and grants listed in NIH's Computer Retrieval of Information on Scientific Projects (CRISP), we conducted our own search of CRISP. Using only the key phrase "chronic fatigue syndrome" for years 1997 through 1999, we searched CRISP and found a number of studies that were not included in the lists of grants originally provided to us by NIH.

NIH officials explained this discrepancy. Projects identified through CRISP are based on text word searching and, as such, are not verified as rigorously as are projects for budget and research reporting, including the CFS grant tables provided to us. Due to the indexing terms used for CRISP and the search logic employed, it is not unusual to observe differences between CRISP-generated lists (which are designed for public access) and formal agency reporting related to fiscal responsibility. According to agency officials, the primary reason for differences between the list of projects found through CRISP and the list of projects reported by the institutes is that the methods used to compile the lists are different. Entering a set of key words in CRISP will generate a list of projects based on the grant application. The institutes may use CRISP as a starting point, but the institutes have procedures to ensure that they report to the budget office only actually funded projects or subprojects. For example, in a large center grant, the CRISP database may include a number of subprojects. Some, but not all, of these subprojects may be related to the specific disease area in question. Occasionally, a planned subproject will not be funded. Such a subproject would not be included in the list of projects generated by the institute but could remain in the CRISP database (see table 2).

ıle 2: NIH Disposition of Projects Identified by CRISP From 1997 Through 1999 Not Included in NIH's List

d disposition	Number
·jects should have been included	
ıall business innovative research grants (grants were not included in NIH's search for CFS grants)	1
ınts funded for a year in addition to that included on the list of projects provided by NIH	1
ɔproject of a general clinical research centers grant	4
ɔproject of a biomedical resource grant	1
ınts inadvertently not included in NIH list, identified by NIH prior to this request	1
·jects were appropriately not included	
S was not the primary focus of the grant	6
ɔproject of a grant, funding of subproject reported in funding of overall project	1
ɔperative Research Center (subproject reported in CRISP by a different title than by NIH)	6
ıect in CRISP had a different title than that on list provided by NIH	2
ɛect number duplicated an earlier grant	1
ɛect was not funded during one of the years for which it was listed in CRISP	1

Tables 3 through 6 list all CFS-related NIH-funded grants and projects, which are administered through the following institutes:

- National Cancer Institute (NCI),
- National Center for Research Resources (NCRR),
- National Heart, Lung, and Blood Institute (NHLBI),
- National Institute of Allergy and Infectious Diseases (NIAID),
- National Institute of Arthritis and Musculoskeletal and Skin Diseases (NIAMS),
- National Institute of Child Health and Human Development (NICHD),
- National Institute of Mental Health (NIMH), and
- National Institute of Neurological Disorders and Stroke (NINDS).

Table 3: NIH-Funded R01 (Research Project) Grants Related to CFS

Fiscal year(s)	Institute	Grant title	Total funding doll.
1987-1990	NIAID	Definition of the Chronic Epstein-Barr Virus Syndrome	$540,2
1989-1991	NIAID	Prevalence of CFS	930,
1990-1992	NIAID	Neuroimmunologic Studies of CFS	871,
1992-1994	NIAID	Chronic Fatigue in Lyme Disease	744,
1992-1994	NIMH	Predictors of Recovery From Acute Viral Infection[a]	716,
1993-1997	NIAID	Human JHK Virus[b]	769,
1993-1995	NIAID	Exertion-Induced Cytokines in CFS[b]	536,
1993-1995, 1997-1999	NIAID	Motor Control and Cytokines in CFS (later retitled Motor Control in CFS)[b]	970,
1993-1995	NIAID	Exercise Intolerance in CFS	454,
1993-1999	NIMH	Research Center on the Psychobiology of Ethnicity[c]	6,978,
1993	NIAID	Virology Assessment of CFS Patients[d]	6,
1993-1996	NIAID	Antigens of Human Herpesvirus-6	521,
1994-1996	NIAID	Virology and Immunology of CFS[b]	497,
1994-1996, 1998-1999	NIAID	Mechanisms of Immunologically Mediated Fatigue	1,008,
1995-1999	NIAID	Estimating Rates of CFS in a Community Sample	2,714,
1995	NCI	Transforming Domain of Human Herpesvirus-6 That Transactivates HIV 1	207,
1995	NCI	Epidemiologic Study of Pediatric HIV-Related Lymphomas	55,
1995	NCI	Molecular Studies on Bovine Immunodeficiency Virus and Bovine Herpes Virus Interactions	21,
1996-1998	NIMH	Cognitive Dysfunction in CFS	275,
1996-1999	NIAID	Dysregulated 2-5A Synthetase/RNase L/PKR Pathways in CFS[e]	1,086,
1996-1998	NIAID	A Trial of Fludrocortisone for CFS[b]	748,
1997-1999	NIAID	Autoantibodies to Cellular Matrix Antigens in CFS	1,063,
1997-1999	NIAID	Mechanisms of Rhinitis in CFS	508,
1998-1999	NIAID	A Model for Induction of CFS	641
1998-1999	NHLBI	Circulatory Control in Young People with Chronic Fatigue	859
1998-1999	NHLBI	Investigation of Orthostatic Intolerance in CFS	639
1998-1999	NIAMS	HPA Axis Dysregulation in Fibromyalgia	385
1999	NIMH	Auditory Working Memory in CFS: A Functional Magnetic Resonance Imaging Study	135
1999	NHLBI	Muscle Blood Flow and CFS	114
1999	NINDS	Motor Learning in CFS: Implications for Neural Dysfunction	160
Total funds			**$25,162**

^aThis NIMH grant was funded prior to the time when NIMH was a part of NIH, but the project extended into the period after which NIMH was a part of NIH. Therefore it is included.

^bGrant funded through selective pay program.

^c This NIMH project studies a range of issues and only a small portion of the funds are spent on CFS-related activities.

^dFrom 1991 through 1995, this project was also a subproject to a cooperative research center project (see table 5). During fiscal year 1993, the project was also supported with an R01-type Research Project grant.

^eThe first-year funding for this grant was under exploratory/developmental grants.

Table 4: NIH-Funded Intramural Research Projects Related to CFS

Fiscal year(s)	Institute	Grant title	Total funding in dollars
1987-1988	NIAID	Study of Sporadic Neurasthenia Associated With Epstein-Barr Virus	$928,400
1989-1996	NIAID	Chronic Epstein-Barr Virus Infection and CFS	6,001,482
1991-1995	NINDS	Neuropsychological Investigations of Human Cognition and Mood State	30,234
1991-1993, 1995	NIMH	CNS Role in the Susceptibility to Inflammatory Illness	428,000
1992-1993	NINDS	Combined Clinical, Viral, and Immunological Studies of Neuromuscular Diseases	6,125
1993-1994	NCI	Epidemiology Studies and Basic Research Related to CFS Outbreaks and Characterization of the Viruses Associated With CFS	399,000
1993-1994	NCI	Support for Physicians Treating CFS Patients by the National Physicians Advisory Group	706,000
1993, 1995-1999	NIMH	Neurobiology of Unipolar Depression	1,033,808
1994, 1998	NICHD	Dose-Response Relationships for Single Doses of Recombinant Human Interleukin-6 in Normal Volunteers and in Patients With Disorders of the Hypothalamic-Pituitary-Adrenal Axis	30,000
1995	NCI	Identification of Human Genetic Loci Which Influence Susceptibility to HIV	115,000
1995	NCI	Regulation of Viral and Cellular Gene Expression	30,000
1995	NCI	Genetic Variation in Infected Hemophiliacs Over Time	30,000
1997-1998	NIAID	Multidisciplinary Studies of CFS	1,795,181
1997-1999	NIAID	Trial of Fludricortisone for Patients With CFS	524,488
Total funds			$12,057,718

Table 5: NIH-Funded Grants and Projects Not Including R01 (Research Project) Grants and Intramural Projects Related to CFS

Fiscal year(s)	Institute	Grant title	Total funding i dollar
1987-1996	NIAID	Pathogenesis of Epstein-Barr Virus Infections	$2,896,62
1989	NCRR	Prevalence of CFS in Ambulatory Medicine	3,94
1989	NCRR	Immunologic and Virologic Studies of CFS	18
1990	NCRR	Sleep and Cytokines in CFS	21,17
1990	NCRR	Involvement of a Human Retrovirus in CFS	8,53
1990	NCRR	Analysis of Clinical and Biological Characterization of CFS	35
1991	NCRR	Psychology and Immunology of CFS and Other Disorders With Severe Fatigue	2,60
1991	NCRR	Acute Experience: Stress and Immune Function in CFS Patients	3,44
1991-1992	NCRR	Ampligen in Patients With CFS and Associated Encephalopathy	103,58
1992-1993	NCRR	Electroencephalogram Sleep in CFS	6,17
1993-1996	NCRR	Exertion Induced Cytokines in CFS	147,88
1993, 1996	NIAID	Coordinating Center for Clinical and Epidemiologic Studies in Infectious Diseases	21,56
1993-1997	NIAID	Social Processes and Somatization—The Course of CFS	625,46
1993, 1995-1999	NCRR	Phosphocreatine Recovery in Women With CFS	111,80
1994-1995	NIAMS	Cytotoxic T Lymphocyte Mediated Cutaneous Immunity to Melanoma	185,39
1994-1995	NIAMS	Molecular Basis of T-Cell Helper Function	92,6
1994-1995	NIAMS	Molecular Determinants of Epstein-Barr Virus Tropism	171,20
1995-1996	NCRR	Neuropsychological Disturbance in CFS	65,5
1995-1997, 1999	NCRR	Exercise Intolerance in CFS	44,02
1995	NCI	Viruses and Oncogenes in Hematopoietic Malignancies	102,0
1996	NCRR	In Vitro Effects of Interleukin 2 on Activity of Natural Killer Cells in CFS	2
1990	NIAID	Operations and Technical Support	444,6
1996	NCRR	Clinical Application of Deoxymyoglobin Technique: Peripheral Vascular Disease or CFS	28,7
1996	NIAID	1996 Scientific and Clinical Meeting, CFS	2,0
1996	NCRR	Microbial Genomic Sequencing in Emerging Disease With Unknown Etiology: Kawasaki, CFS	121,3
1997-1998	NCRR	Hypothalamic-Pituitary-Adrenal Axis Dysregulation in Fibromyalgia	130,8
1997	NCRR	Comparative Study of Pathophysiologic Descriptors of CFS	1,9
1997-1998	NCRR	Trial of Fludrocortisone for CFS	25,1
1997-1998	NCRR	Regulation of Adrenal Function in Fibromyalgia	129,6
1997	NCRR	Immunoneuroendocrine Response to Tetanus Toxoid	19,6
1998	NCRR	Psychiatric Diagnosis and Biological Markers in Neuresthenia, CFS, and Depression	18,5

ntinued From Previous Page)

cal year(s)	Institute	Grant title	Total funding in dollars
98	NIAID	CFS in Adolescents, Workshops	12,855
99	NCRR	Mitochondria in CFS Pathology	178
99	NCRR	Models for Induction of CFS	18,933
99	NCRR	Psychoimmunological and Neuroendocrinological Response	315
99	NCRR	Mechanisms of Rhinitis in CFS	47,865
99	NCRR	Skeletal Muscle in Persian Gulf Veterans With CFS	21,009
99	NIAID	Diagnosis and Treatment of CFS	250,000
99	NIAID	Venous Dysfunction in CFS	73,247
99	NIAID	Siberian Ginseng for the Treatment of CFS	67,827
al funds			$6,029,109

Table 6: NIAID Cooperative Research Center Projects Related to CFS

Fiscal year(s)	Grant title	Total funding doll.
Brigham and Women's Hospital (1991-1995)		
1991-94	CFS, Fybromyalgia, and Depression	$949,3
1991-94	Cytokines and CFS	543,2
1995	Core A	100,0
National Jewish Center for Immunology/Resp. Med. (1992-1995)		
1992-94	Clinical Research on CFS and Quantification of Fatigue	411,6
1992-94	Developmental Research on CFS and Quantification of Fatigue	56,2
1992-95	Quantification of Fatigue in CFS	307,4
1992-95	Allergic Inflammatory Reactions in CFS	414,1
1992-95	Neurophysiologic Disturbance in CFS	486,3
1992-95	Neuropsychiatric Features of CFS	374,6
University of Medicine and Dentistry of New Jersey (1991-1995, 1995-1998, 1999-present)		
1991-95	Classification of CFS Patients	1,533,
1991-95	Virology Assessment of CFS Patients	568,
1991-94	Immunological Assessment of CFS Patients	586,
1995-98	Administrative and Data Analysis Core	841,
1995-98	Categorization of CFS Patients	1,675,
1995-98	Exercise, Fatigue, and Training	1,209,
1999	Brain and Cardiovascular Studies	302,
1999	Physiological Challenges in CFS	203,
1999	Statistical and Data Core	238,
University of Washington (1995-1998, 1999-present)		
1995-00	Clinical Core	321,
1995-98	CFS: Neuropsychological, Neuroendocrine, Sleep Function	493,
1995-98	Immunology and Virology of CFS in Monozygotic Twins	662,
1995-98	Biological/Psychosocial Factors: Post-Infectious Fatigue	490,
1995-98	Prognosis of CFS	525,
1999	Monozygotic Twins With CFS—Predisposition of Perception	269
1999	Population Based Twin Study of CFS	202,
1999	Biostatistical and Data Management	140,
1999	Children of CFS Patients	140,

(Continued From Previous Page)

Fiscal year(s)	Grant title	Total funding in dollars
University of Miami (1999-present)		
1999	Cognitive-Behavioral Stress Management Intervention for CFS	136,299
1999	Effect of Stress and Cognitive-Behavioral Stress Management on Natural Killer Activity in CFS	61,147
1999	Laboratory Assessment	153,311
Total funds		$14,399,965

Congressionally Requested CFS Activities for CDC and NIH

CDC Response to Congressional Committee Requests for CFS Activities

CDC has initiated work on most CFS activities requested in congressional committee report language. However, procedures for ensuring that the branch chiefs responsible for the work were aware of congressional expectations have only recently been established. Agency officials reported that while CDC has distributed to the centers the relevant portions from House, Senate, and conference appropriations reports, it has only been since the arrival of an associate director for management at the Division of Viral and Rickettsial Diseases in 1997 that this report language has been disseminated to the division's branch chiefs responsible for planning the research.

Of the 33 requested CFS activities, 3 are planned for this fiscal year (see table 7). CDC reports that it plans to initiate a national survey in 2000, but is unclear that this will include a surveillance component as suggested in congressional committee reports in 1998. CDC also reports it will begin planning for the establishment of a CFS patient registry in fiscal year 2000 as suggested by report language in 1991. This patient registry will also allow CDC to address the third area of congressional interest, suggested in 1997: developing a CFS brain tissue repository.

Table 7: Congressionally Requested CFS Activities for CDC

Activity requested	Year(s) requested	Year(s) started
Develop and implement a surveillance network.	1988	19
Expand surveillance system to all states.	1988	
Increase level of research support.	1988	198
Work with Nevada.	1988	19
Expand sentinel surveillance.	1989, 1990	19
Expand study on link between CFS and human herpesvirus-6.	1989	19
Continue attempts to detect persistent virus infections in CFS patients and to develop appropriate controls.	1989	19
Expand surveillance to Nevada.	1989	19
Enroll patients in case studies.	1990	19
Investigate suspected clusters.	1990	19
Train and educate physicians and health workers about CFS.	1990, 1998	19
Develop information for the general public to increase the general understanding of CFS.	1990	19
Expand research on immunologic abnormalities.	1990	19
Provide CFS information, outreach, conference, and training activities.	1991	19
Refine CFS definition.	1991	19

ontinued From Previous Page)

tivity requested	Year(s) requested	Year(s) started
dy the establishment of a CFS patient registry.	1991	2000[c]
velop recommendations to the U.S. biomedical community on standardized clinical data ection instruments and procedures for evaluating functional health status in CFS.	1991, 1992	1994
ise on the establishment of standardized protocols for CFS laboratory tests.	1991, 1992	1994
re serum and leucocyte samples from CFS patients for future testing.	1991, 1992	1992
and immunological, virological, and toxicological studies of CFS.	1993	1992
and CFS research activities, including research on the relationship of CFS to pregnancy, a study FS patients in remission to monitor the long-term effects of the disease, and research on the act of CFS on health professionals.	1993	1994[d]
ke available to interested parties preliminary and pending data related to the CFS surveillance em, data from the case-control study that began in June 1992, and data related to CDC onses to cluster outbreaks of CFS.	1993	1990[e]
and the surveillance system to 8- to 18-year-olds	1993	1992
duct community-based prevalence studies to collect data on endemic cases and possible ter outbreaks and to document the basic epidemiology of CFS.	1995	1993
port four studies on possible transmission routes, especially among health care workers, family mbers, and maternal transmission to unborn children.	1995, 1996	[f]
vide education programs, as appropriate.	1995, 1996	1997
nplete and expand current CFS surveillance projects.	1996	1996
mmence a case-control phase of the community-based surveillance study recently completed in Francisco.	1996	1997[g]
sider implementing the review panel's recommendations, particularly in the areas of etiology ies and brain tissue repositories.	1997	1996, 2000[h]
ance CFS laboratory studies and surveillance projects, including outreach to populations not iously recognized as being affected by CFS, especially minorities, children, and adolescents.	1998, 1999	1997
ourage continuation and expansion of studies of adolescents and children.	1998	1993
a neuroendocrinologist to research group.	1998, 1999	1999[i]
ate studies on rates of CFS among health care workers, family members of CFS patients, and nant women.	1998	1994[d]

[a]National survey planned for 2000.

[b]Funding levels show an increase since 1988.

[c]Meeting planned.

[d]Does not include pregnant women.

[e]Findings presented.

[f]CDC has found no evidence that CFS is transmissible.

[g]Data used as pilot of Wichita study.

[h]Etiology studies began in 1996; brain tissue repositories in 2000.

[i]Hiring in process.

Within these activities, however, CDC is not pursuing or considers infeasible the following areas of congressional interest: investigating the relationship of CFS to pregnancy (part of an activity requested in 1993); supporting four studies of possible transmission routes (requested in 199 and 1996); commencing a new phase of the community-based surveillanc study completed in San Francisco that compared CFS patients to healthy controls (requested in 1996); and initiating studies on the rates of CFS among pregnant women (part of an activity requested in 1998). CDC reported justifications for a number of these unaddressed areas. For example, the agency has not conducted and does not anticipate studying pregnant women because the low age-specific prevalence rate suggests that pregnant women would rarely be affected and human subjects and ethical considerations preclude such studies. Further, while it has conducted studies of transmission since 1985, the agency was not aware the four transmission studies referred to in the report language. Finally, while the San Francisco study was used as a pilot for the Wichita surveillance study, CDC reported that it was not possible to compare CF patients with healthy individuals in San Francisco due to the nature of th study.

NIH Response to Congressional Committee Requests for CFS Activities

NIH has been asked to pursue CFS work in 34 areas by congressional appropriations committees (see table 8). Five activities have not been pursued or are considered by NIH to be infeasible: expand research in identification of eventual cure (requested in 1988); expand research on genetic disposition and allergy, immune and neurological systems (requested in 1991); designate reference laboratories for CFS (requested 1991); compile a CFS patient registry (requested in 1992); and address ca needs, including the education of providers in assessment, diagnosis an treatment, case management, and rehabilitative efforts (requested in 199

NIH reported that all CFS research efforts are designed to find an event cure. However, because so little is currently known about CFS, the agen has not reported any specific activities directly related to a cure (althou it has initiated some studies of possible treatments) or to direct linkage between genetic disposition and allergy, immune, and neurological systems. NIH considered establishing a CFS patient registry but determined that it was not feasible and that it was more part of CDC's purview. Finally, NIH reported to the appropriations committees that th language regarding care needs was more appropriate for HHS' Health Resources and Services Administration.

able 8: Congressionally Requested CFS Activities for NIH

ctivity requested	Year(s) requested	Year started
xpand research in search for a diagnostic technique.	1988	1992
crease efforts to discover cause and treatments.	1988, 1994	1991
xpand research in identification of an eventual cure.	1988	
onsider use of the small grants program for research on the chronic Epstein-Barr virus syndrome.	1988	1991
ocate additional research in Nevada.	1989	1991
onduct research on understanding and correcting immune system damage.	1990	1991
udy the feasibility of establishing a research center for CFS studies, including collecting and nalyzing clinical and laboratory data on patients.	1990	1991
sue a request for applications on CFS to increase the number of extramural research grants funded.	1990	1991
licit and fund additional research grants.	1991	1991
tiate a consortium of research centers for CFS research, preferably at the Universities of Nevada d Minnesota.	1991	1992
xpand research with other institutes.	1991	1991
xpand biomedical meetings.	1991	1992
crease extramural and intramural research studies.	1991	1991
eport annually to the Congress on activities related to CFS.	1991, 1992, 1993	1991
onduct a conference in fiscal year 1991 on NIH activities related to CFS.	1991	1991
pand research on genetic predisposition and allergy, immune, and neurological systems.	1991	
esignate reference laboratories and facilitate data exchange among institutions in the geographic eas in which CFS concentrates.	1991	
esignate a senior agency official to act as CFS coordinator.	1991	1991
tablish a multidisciplinary study section for CFS.	1992, 1993	1993
tablish a standing study section for CFS.	1993	1993
mpile a CFS patient registry.	1992	
idy the feasibility of establishing a central clearinghouse for CFS data .	1992	1992
ike grants to, or enter into contracts with, public or nonprofit entities for the development and eration of centers to conduct basic and clinical research on CFS.	1993	1993
sure that individuals who have expertise in CFS or neuromuscular diseases and are representative a variety of disciplines and fields are appointed to appropriate NIH advisory committees and ards.	1993, 1998, 1999	1993
tablish procedures to enable the patient community to provide input to the direction of CFS search at NIH.	1993	1993
nsider increasing opportunities for CFS patients and researchers to participate in advisory mmittees.	1993	1993
nduct studies that continue to look into retrovirus activity and other areas of infectious disease thogenesis.	1994	1994

(Continued From Previous Page)

Activity requested	Year(s) requested	Year started
Direct resources to extramural grants focused on promising areas of biomedical research and to investigations seeking to identify etiological agents and markers for the pathophysiology of CFS.	1996, 1998	199
Appoint a CFS coordinator with NIAID-wide authority.	1996, 1998	199
Include other agencies, such as CDC and HHS' Health Resources and Services Administration, in the planning and execution of the workshop on pediatric CFS.	1998	199
Recommend that the Office of Research on Women's Health develop a strategy to address chronic pain syndromes in women.	1998	199
Use all mechanisms, including program announcements, to study all facets of pediatric CFS.	1999	19
Address care needs, including the education of providers in assessment, diagnosis and treatment, case management, and rehabilitative efforts.	1999	
Establish chronic fatigue assessment and treatment centers.	1999	199

[a]Workshop.

[b]Recompeted.

External Review Recommendations to CDC and NIH

Recommendations to DC

CDC's 1996 peer review, conducted by four scientists and two patient advocates, noted that considerable progress had been made, specifically outlining some strengths of the CFS program. The review team recognized CDC's critical leadership role in the development of a case definition, the valuable studies the agency had conducted on the rate of recovery from CFS, and the agency's effort to study retroviral agents as a cause of CFS. The report also included several recommendations: four general recommendations, nine recommendations related to work conducted up to that time, three recommendations related to proposed future studies, and two recommendations related to possible additional research areas. For the most part, CDC has undertaken activities in response to these recommendations. (See table 9.)

le 9: Recommendations From CDC's 1996 Peer Review and Agency Response

:ommendation	CDC response
heral recommendations	
C's CFS team should enhance its communications and aboration with NIH; NIH should regularly inform CDC about oing progress and the results of both its intramural and its amural research programs on CFS, and CDC should regularly rm NIH about ongoing progress and the results of its ongoing lies. It appears that HHS' CFS Coordinating Committee SCC) concentrates primarily on discussing the intramural earch programs at NIH and CDC.	CDC and NIH regularly provide updates to members of CFSCC and attendees at that meeting regarding their respective CFS programs.
C's CFS program should be regularly reviewed by an external ew group.	Subsequent to this 1996 review, CDC's CFS program was reviewed in 1999—the most recent external peer review.
vided the Viral Exanthems and Herpesvirus Branch can elop additional expertise in the fields of neuroendocrinology neuropsychology, the placement of the CFS program within branch continues to be appropriate.	The Viral Exanthems and Herpesvirus Branch is developing expertise in neuroendocrinology and neuropsychology through agreements with Emory University.
C's CFS program should continue its ongoing active dialogue patient advocacy groups.	Meeting held at CDC in October 1999.
ommendations related to program accomplishments to date	
istical techniques, such as cluster analysis and discriminant tion analysis, should be used to assess the robustness of ngs related to case definition, and these same statistical niques (including factor analysis) should be applied to other sets as they emerge.	Standard operating procedure.
stigations of potential clusters of cases should begin as early ossible after the onset of the putative outbreak to ensure the est likelihood of identifying an etiologic agent.	Program begins investigations of reported clusters as early as possible. Emphasis in both cluster investigations and population studies is to detect and study incident CFS cases.

(Continued From Previous Page)

Recommendation	CDC response
CDC should write a formal assessment of the reasons for the considerable differences in the observed prevalence rates from different studies, besides differences in the completeness of the case ascertainment techniques across the studies.	Done in discussion of newest prevalence manuscript to be submitted for publication.
CDC should comment on the possible biological implications of some of the differences in prevalence it has observed in different age, gender, and socioeconomic groups.	Done in discussions of all appropriate manuscripts.
Future studies should focus on prevalence in children and geriatric populations. Widely repeated anecdotal evidence indicates that teachers, airline workers, and health care workers may be differently affected. (To some extent, such possible occupational associations have been evaluated already in the San Francisco study, but it is not clear whether the sample size of this cross-sectional observational study allowed confident conclusions.)	—Wichita surveillance includes all residents 2 years and older. —The National Survey (planned for fall 2000) will give special emphasis to children. —The National Survey will collect detailed information on possible occupational associations with CFS.
CDC should continue some studies of the possible role of human herpesvirus 6 in CFS. The group strongly supports further study of Borna disease virus. CDC should also study the relationship of other known or newly-discovered microorganisms that could, on the basis of their association with other similar illnesses or their tissue tropism, be potential triggering agents or cofactors for CFS.	—CDC's most recent study of the possible associations between CFS and human herpesvirus 6 and 7 found no association. —CDC supported additional studies of Borna disease virus, which found no association with CFS. —The Viral Exanthems and Herpesvirus Branch is developing expertise in identification and characterization of novel infectious agents possibly associated with CFS.
A regular formal process should be instituted for reviewing and updating information for the public. In particular, these updates should reflect all published research, whether conducted at CDC or elsewhere.	Standard operating procedure for CDC programs. Program does n have resources to maintain and disseminate data on all published CFS research.
CDC's Internet web site should include a written summary of all programs and all work on CFS currently under way at CDC. Printed copies of the information should be available to those who do not have access to the Internet. The web site might also contain a "Hot Topic" button that provides brief, timely statements about CFS-related issues that have been highly visible in the media.	—The web site now includes a summary of all new CDC work on CFS. —Printed copies of information are available to those without Internet access. CDC operates a CFS voice information system th offers the option of receiving printed materials. CDC also provides such information in response to written queries. — The web site contains a Hot Topics button.
Each public document about CFS and each public presentation and media interview about CFS should state clearly and prominently that CFS is a "priority one emerging illness."	NCID no longer uses this classification.

Recommendations related to proposed future studies

Some follow-up beyond a 1-year review in Wichita should be planned with at least a sample of the cases (and noncases) identified during the initial year. The study should attempt to assess the level of debility/functional status in this population. The study should also follow a sample of patients who report debilitating chronic fatigue but who do not fully meet CDC's case definition of CFS.	—Approximately 8,000 subjects who completed detailed interview during the initial survey have been followed for 3 years. In addition monitoring the clinical courses of the disease, this measures incidence of CFS. —A manuscript describing functional status at baseline is in preparation. Following the third year of follow-up, analyses will explore functional status over time.
The representational difference analysis technique should be used not only with peripheral mononuclear cells but also with tissue specimens and cerebrospinal fluid, when possible.	—Program determined after review that this technique was not th most appropriate method and is using other strategies. —At present, only peripheral blood cells can be collected from subjects enrolled in population-based studies.

(Continued From Previous Page)

Recommendation	CDC response
studies of stress and herpes simplex virus 1 reactivation should not be supported.	Herpes simplex virus 1 reactivation protocol was stopped.
Recommendations related to possible additional research areas	
CDC should develop some collaborations with neuroendocrinologists to study the hypothalamic-pituitary axis.	Neuroendocrinologist should be on staff (through agreement with Emory) by September 2000.
CDC could provide an international service by offering to create a brain bank of specimens available for study, including other tissue specimens from these same patients, when possible.	CDC will convene a meeting in fall 2000 to initiate this process.

Source: Recommendations from "External Peer Review of the Chronic Fatigue Syndrome Research Program," August 1996. CDC responses reported to GAO.

Subsequent to the 1996 review, CDC underwent a 1999 peer review and a review of the Board of Scientific Counselors. These two concurrent reviews had a consistent message: CDC should look for more opportunities to collaborate. Specifically, the reviews suggested that NIH researchers work with some of the tissue samples obtained by CDC from the Wichita study. The peer review also suggested that there be more professional education efforts. CDC has many activities planned to address these recommendations (see table 10).

Table 10: Recommendations From CDC's 1999 Peer Review, Board of Scientific Counselor Review, and Meeting With Patient Advocates, and Agency Response

Recommendations	CDC response
General recommendations	
Broaden collaborations.	Collaborations vary depending on program at the time.
Broaden communication with Council of State and Territorial Epidemiologists, advocates.	In process.
Broaden availability of patients and specimens to scientific community.	Standard operating procedure, depending on program strategy and priorities and the quality of proposals.
Recommendations related to surveillance	
Continue Wichita cohort beyond 3 years.	Clinical cohort time frame extended.
Study quality of life, economic burden, patient management, long-term care, and behavioral and functional sequelae.	A manuscript is being drafted, and CDC is hiring a medical research officer and conducting clinical studies. CDC also plans to conduct a national survey.
Explore CFS in families and occupations.	A manuscript is being drafted, and CDC plans to conduct a national survey.
Place more emphasis on adolescents.	CDC is welcoming a pediatrician to complete a sabbatical year at CDC; adolescents will be studied in the national survey.
Use the modified case definition in future studies.	Standard operating procedure.

(Continued From Previous Page)

Recommendations	CDC response
Recommendations related to case definition	
Consider revising case definition.	A workshop was conducted in May 2000 to consider this topic.
Use factor analysis on other databases.	In process; planned as part of the May 2000 workshop.
Measure chronic unwellness in the national survey.	Survey will be designed to capture such data.
Use factor scores (chronic unwellness) to better weight symptoms and measure severity.	In process and part of the national survey.
Recommendations related to clinical studies	
Recruit a medical research officer.	In process.
Convene a review group for endocrine studies.	In process.
Design protocols for neuropsychological studies combined with brain imaging.	Exploring this with Emory University.
Recommendations related to molecular epidemiology	
Improve balance of gene expression analysis program.	In process.
Develop a program to search for novel uncharacterized infectious agents.	Was part of the April 2000 Banbury Conference, *Strategies for Identification and Characterization of Unknown Pathogens*, which CDC co-organized and cosponsored.
Recognize CFS as a contagious disease that occurs in clusters.	Clusters are examined on request, but CFS does not appear to be contagious.
Assess risk of transfusion transmission.	A statement regarding risk has been released, and CDC continues to monitor.
Broaden investigations to consider environmental exposures/toxicology.	There is no evidence from CDC's case control studies to support this, but the agency continues to monitor.
Recommendations related to education (focus on health care providers should continue)	
Maintain web page.	Done.
Develop continuing medical education materials.	In process with HHS' Health Resources and Services Administration.
Develop national CFS information campaign.	CDC maintains a web page, publishes journal articles, and provides other information.
React to CFS articles in reviewed journals and in popular press.	Standard operating procedure, when appropriate.
Explore CFS education in schools and establish liaison with the Department of Education.	Will follow up, as appropriate.

Source: Recommendations from CDC. CDC responses reported to GAO.

Recommendations to NIH

NIAID's National Advisory Allergy and Infectious Diseases Council meets about three times a year and occasionally has discussed NIH's CFS program. In conjunction with those discussions, the council has sometime made recommendations to that program. In February 1993, the council advocated that NIH support specific studies suggested by findings from case demographics. At its February/March 1994 meeting, the council concurred with the need and desirability of continuing and expanding the CFS Cooperative Research Centers program and reapproved the centers then and again in September 1997. In September 1995, the Division of Microbiology and Infectious Diseases subcommittee of the council more formally assessed the CFS program and determined that NIAID should retain overall leadership of NIH's CFS efforts but that a multidisciplinary research approach should also continue, involving other institutes where appropriate. At the next council meeting, in May 1996, the division asked for and obtained approval of a program announcement on CFS, supported by eight institutes and offices. The subcommittee noted that the initiative was responsive to its recommendation to both explore new hypotheses of causes and disease development and to involve other NIH entities in the CFS research effort. The subcommittee also had a number of specific scientific suggestions. The areas of study that were recommended included consideration of multiple disease causes, studies of patients with shorter duration of illness, longitudinal studies of immune markers correlated with clinical findings, information about factors predictive of recovery and recovery rates, the use of tissue samples to test theories involving certain cell alterations, issues related to pregnancy, and epidemiological research into CFS in children and adolescents. NIH has conducted investigations in all but two of these areas (studies of patients with shorter duration of illness and issues related to pregnancy).

NIH also has an internal coordinating committee for CFS comprised of representatives from all relevant and interested institutes within the agency. While this might have been intended initially to serve as a forum for intraagency communication, it has instead, according to agency officials, more recently served as a way of providing information for use at the meetings of HHS' CFSCC. Further, attendance at the meetings has been optional, and agency officials reported that representatives from those institutes that have small programs with only one or two grants rarely attend.

NIH Expenditures on CFS Research, by Institute and Center

Fiscal year	NCI	NCRR[a]	NHLBI	NIAID	NIAMS[a]	NICHD[a]	NIMH[b]	NINDS[a]	Tot
1987	$0	$0	$0	$782	$0	$0	$0	$0	$7
1988	0	0	0	988	0	0	0	0	9
1989	0	4	0	1,472	0	0	0	0	1,4
1990	0	30	0	1,793	0	0	0	0	1,8
1991	0	25	0	2,710	0	0	112	15	2,8
1992	0	86	0	2,978	0	0	417	11	3,4
1993	550	38	0	3,841	0	0	1,311	6	5,7
1994	555	56	0	4,226	218	10	1,107	4	6,1
1995	560	103	0	5,252	231	0	1,226	1	7,4
1996	0	249	0	4,984	0	0	1,341	0	6,5
1997	0	222	0	4,966	0	0	1,491	0	6,6
1998	0	134	819	4,233	176	20	1,406	0	6,7
1999	0	138	794	4,434	209	0	1,156	161	6,8

Note: Dollars in thousands.

[a]Funding for institutes' and centers' projects was below NIH threshold for disease reporting of $250,000. Because of our review, institutes and centers were asked to more carefully examine their CFS project funding. Nevertheless, there may be a slight underreporting of CFS funding.

[b]NIMH reported total funding for a CFS center project, consistent with its policy to report entire projects. Following additional review, NIH determined that only a portion of the project was related CFS.

[c]Due to rounding, figures in total column may not be the sum of institutes' and centers' yearly expenditures.

NIH Activities in Support of CFS Research

NIH has issued four program announcements to stimulate research on CFS. The first, a program announcement initiated by NIAID in 1987, targeted studies in the epidemiology of CFS and chronic Epstein-Barr virus infection to advance understanding of the prevalence, causes, and natural history of these syndromes.[1] In 1992, NIAID initiated a program announcement that called for applications to explore biologically rational hypotheses concerning exercise-induced fatigue and/or disease origin and development in CFS patients. In 1994, NIH issued its first joint program announcement—with NIAID, NIAMS, and NIMH—calling for studies on the causes, natural history, and origin and development of CFS. This announcement listed 10 different areas that merited further study, including low levels of cortisol, sleep disturbance, demographic risk factors, and increased frequency of psychiatric diagnoses in CFS patients. The most recent program announcement was issued in 1996 and involved eight different units within NIH. This program announcement was designed to support studies of CFS' functional effects on the body, ideally addressing new hypotheses and research gaps, or small studies exploring new ideas. This program announcement listed 23 areas needing additional research.[2]

NIH officials told us they established a CFS Special Emphasis Panel for the review of CFS grant applications for a number of reasons, including demonstrating the agency's commitment to CFS research, because CFS is little understood and because so few applications for CFS were being received. The panels were designed to help facilitate consideration and scoring of CFS grant applications that might otherwise not receive scores favorable enough to be funded if reviewed by a standing study section. Members are selected for a special emphasis panel after grant applications are received so that those with appropriate expertise are appointed to serve as reviewers. Like all review panels, members of the CFS Special Emphasis Panel are external researchers, not employees of NIH. An NIH official told us that most applications that have gone to the CFS Special Emphasis Panel have received better scores than they would have if they had gone to a standing study section. At the National Advisory Allergy and Infectious Diseases Council meeting in February 1993, the chief of the Virology Branch commented that the application review process had

---

[1]At the time, some experts believed there might be a relationship between CFS and Epstein-Barr virus.

[2]These areas included overlapping symptomatology with neurally mediated hypotension, the role of cardiovascular regulatory centers, role of neuroendocrine and neuroimmune functions, hormonal effects, and the role of environmental agents.

improved significantly since the establishment of a special emphasis panel for CFS. To date, of the applications reviewed by the CFS Special Emphasis Panel, a total of 30 extramural grants (R01 grants, or research projects) have been funded. (See app. IV.)

The CFS Special Emphasis Panel was designed to help improve the chances of CFS grants getting funded. During fiscal years 1988 through 1999, the funding rate for CFS was 24.32 percent versus 28.31 percent for all grants across the same institutes that fund CFS research. It is plausible that the quality of CFS applications has been inferior to the quality of those in other areas, accounting for the lower rates. It is also plausible that this rate of funding is indeed higher than it would have been had the applications been reviewed by standing panels.

The agency has used an additional approach for facilitating the funding of CFS research. NIH has a process for all areas of research, called "selective payment," designed to provide funding to a small number of applications that are programmatically important but not rated favorably enough to receive funding. From 1992 through 1996, six CFS applications were funded—all by NIAID—through this process. NIH's description of the selective payment process states that it is designed to support applications that received scores just beyond the funding cut-off; however, the CFS applications funded through this process were, in fact, ranked quite poorly.[3] NIAID appears to have made extra efforts to fund some CFS research.

In addition to these efforts, NIH has issued three requests for applications for CFS Cooperative Research Centers since 1991. The centers are designed to augment the existing grant program and to provide a sustained multidisciplinary approach to CFS research. The intent is to advance the field by bridging the basic science and clinical research arenas and facilitating confirmatory testing and follow-up of new hypotheses and observations. The purpose of the initial request for applications, issued in 1991, was to stimulate the establishment of centers of CFS research excellence in which coordinated projects in the fields of immunology, virology, medicine, and clinical epidemiology could be pursued. These

---

[3]The percentile rankings of all CFS applications funded under the selective payment program ranged from 53.7 to 75—well above what would be expected with just over 28 percent of the applications being funded overall. A high percentile ranking is assigned to applications with poor scores and a low percentile ranking is assigned to those with good scores.

awards were for a period of up to 4 years, with funds set aside for this purpose. NIAID funded three centers with the fiscal year 1991 request for applications, two with the second request in fiscal year 1995, and three with the final request in fiscal year 1999. Under the last request for applications, funds had been set aside for only two centers. However, few CFS grant applications had been funded that year, and we were told that, because the agency wanted to spend money on CFS research, the extra grant funds were used to support a third center.

NIH Grant Process

NIH's institutes and centers award grants to nonprofit and for-profit organizations; institutions of higher education; hospitals; research foundations; governments and their agencies; and, occasionally, individuals. Applications are usually initiated by the principal investigator, signed also by an authorized official of the applicant institution, and these are received by NIH's Center for Scientific Review. Approximately 37,000 grant applications are processed each year. Applications are ordinarily unsolicited, but NIH may encourage the submission of grant applications on particular topics through the use of one of two special devices: program announcements—which describe continuing, new, or expanded program interests—and requests for applications, which invite applications in a well-defined scientific area and for which specific funds have been earmarked and a special review process has been designed.

Within the Center for Scientific Review, all applications that are competing for funds are assigned to a specific institute or center and to an integrated review group. The institute or center chosen is the one that may eventually have the opportunity to fund the research. The review group chosen is the one that would be most appropriate for assessing the scientific merit of the research grant application.

An integrated review group is a chartered organization divided into study sections, each of which is composed of 12 to 20 mostly nonfederal scientists who are selected for their competence and generally serve 4-year terms. These members are sent copies of the relevant applications about 6 weeks before the study section's scheduled meeting; for each application, specific members are chosen to provide written reviews or to act as discussants. A special emphasis panel operates like a study section in that it peer reviews applications, but it is formed on an ad hoc basis, and it reviews applications on only a relatively specific topic.

One week before a study section meets, the Scientific Review
Administrator from the Center for Scientific Review solicits from all
members a list of applications believed not to rank in the top half for
scientific merit. The individual lists are compared and those on all lists a
not discussed at the meeting. At a meeting of the study section, the revie
administrator and a chairperson from the study section jointly conduct t
peer review, which usually lasts 2 days. Observers, such as program staff
from the relevant institutes and centers may attend but do not participat
in the discussions. Reviewers and discussants assigned to an application
provide their evaluations. Then, after a general discussion, members ma
their priority scores privately for each application. Average priority scor
and percentiles are eventually generated for each one as summary
outcomes of this peer review process. The review instructions are the sar
for standing study sections and special emphasis panels.

Applicants are provided with detailed feedback from the study section
meeting in about 6 to 8 weeks, but final decisions about awards depend
further steps centering around a second level of review by the institute's
advisory council. For NIAID, the National Advisory Allergy and Infectiou
Diseases Council conducts this second review. This council and the
equivalent councils or boards in other institutes and centers are
responsible, by law, for the final external review of all grant applications
recommended for further consideration. Its members represent health,
science, and the public. The second level of review is designed to evalua
applications in relation to the needs of the institute or center and the
priorities of its director. The council may concur with the review group (
special emphasis panel) recommendations or it may vote to change the
first-level review recommendations via several different mechanisms. T
can include applications selected for funding under selective payment.
Selective payment requires that an institute or center reserve a portion (
extramural research funds for applications that meet programmatic nee
but are scored at the margin of the pay cut-off. Generally, studies are
identified for selective payment by the institute or center director and a
evaluated by the unit's advisory council.

Comments From the Department of Health and Human Services

DEPARTMENT OF HEALTH & HUMAN SERVICES   Office of Inspector General

Washington, D.C. 20201

MAY 1 8 200

Ms. Janet Heinrich
Associate Director, Health Financing
    and Public Health Issues
United States General
    Accounting Office
Washington, D.C. 20548

Dear Ms. Heinrich:

Enclosed are the Department's comments on your draft report,
"Chronic Fatigue Syndrome: CDC and NIH Research Activities
Broad-Based But Agency Coordination Limited." The comments
represent the tentative position of the Department and are
subject to reevaluation when the final version of this report is
received.

The Department also provided extensive technical comments
directly to your staff.

The Department appreciates the opportunity to comment on this
draft report before its publication.

                          Sincerely,

                          June Gibbs Brown
                          Inspector General

Enclosure

The Office of Inspector General (OIG) is transmitting the
Department's response to this draft report in our capacity as
the Department's designated focal point and coordinator for
General Accounting Office reports. The OIG has not conducted
an independent assessment of these comments and therefore
expresses no opinion on them.

**Comments of the Department of Health and Human Services
on the General Accounting Office Draft Report Entitled
"Chronic Fatigue Syndrome: CDC and NIH Research Activities Broad-Based
But Agency Coordination Limited" GAO/HEHS-00-98**

General Comments

The Department of Health and Human Services (Department) appreciates the opportunity
to comment on the General Accounting Office's (GAO) draft report. In general, we are
pleased that the report accurately conveys the firm commitment of the Department, and in
particular two of the Department's operating divisions; the National Institutes of Health
(NIH) and the Centers for Disease Control and Prevention (CDC), to chronic fatigue
syndrome (CFS) research. In addition, the report describes the many efforts the
Department has made to remove obstacles to research on CFS and also accurately notes
many of the problems faced by the Department's operating divisions in this area. The
Department thanks the GAO for their intense and dedicated efforts in preparing a
thorough, thoughtful report, particularly in identifying the differences and similarities in
operating division approaches to funding CFS research. However, we do believe it is
important to address and clarify a number of issues.

With regard to the Chronic Fatigue Syndrome Coordinating Committee (CFSCC), the
GAO report notes how the Committee could function more effectively as a coherent body
with focus and direction. The Department agrees with these findings, particularly since
the CFSCC is the only formal mechanism in the Department for advocacy groups to have
a direct voice on CFS issues. A considerable amount of time is given to hearing input
from patients and advocates at CFSCC meetings. Although there are many items to be
addressed, updates from operating divisions at CFSCC meetings provide opportunities
for those present, including patients and advocates, to learn what activities and efforts are
currently underway at the Department's operating divisions. It should be noted that the
CFSCC has made progress in a number of areas that is consistent with its goals, including
identifying educational opportunities and developing informed responses to constituency
groups on efforts and progress. The CFSCC has brought together operating divisions
other than CDC and NIH to discuss CFS issues and has begun to address areas such as
physician education and development of medical and other health professional school
curricula on CFS.

See comment 1, p. 73.

The GAO report also mentions that there is a lack of coordination and collaboration
between CDC and NIH. Although avenues may exist for collaborative opportunities, it
should be noted that much of the work funded by these operating divisions is extramural
in nature and that there are few intramural investigators, which may limit direct, internal
collaboration on research activities. The Department wants to emphasize that, while
some readers may get the impression from GAO's report that the level of communication
between CDC and NIH is minimal or sporadic, that is not the case. As with other
diseases within the purview of both CDC and NIH, the vast majority of interactions
between operating divisions for purposes of communication and coordination occur

1

See comment 2, p. 73.

See comment 3, p. 73.

See comment 4, p. 73.

See comment 5, p. 73.

informally at the program level. This is the level at which most of the "work" gets done and this interaction is working well regarding CFS research activities.

In relation to research on CFS, it appears to be the opinion of GAO that NIH has not heeded the concerns of the CFS advocacy community. While it is important to solicit and seriously consider input from patient advocates, advice from these constituencies is only one aspect in deciding the future direction of research in a particular area. Funding decisions for NIH grants are based primarily on the technical merit scores of the applications received and, hence, strategies to increase the quality of applications should be a primary goal in all areas of CFS research. It is also important to note that, while some CFS funds at CDC were not used for CFS activities, only one planned study was not initiated because of insufficient funds. The CDC has since determined that particular study to be methodologically unfeasible.

With respect to project funding, a related issue is the success of NIH's CFS Special Emphasis Panel (SEP) in increasing the number of investigator-initiated CFS grants that receive fundable scores. The GAO report does not distinguish between the plausibility of the hypotheses that the SEP has or has not helped to improve the chances of CFS grants to receive fundable scores. The NIH opinion is emphatically that it has. Scientific research classically involves the collection of objective data to test a hypothesis. Formerly, most CFS research fared poorly in standing study sections as a result of the lack of objective endpoints for scientific investigation. Consequently, aggressive use of the selective pay mechanism was essential to maintain a research program. As the state of knowledge of CFS has not yet advanced significantly as far as identifying quantifiable endpoints, it can be expected that CFS grants would again be at a severe disadvantage in standard study sections.

The Department would also like to clarify another issue where there were patient advocate concerns. Patient advocates state that they were not involved in the planning of a meeting that developed into an NIH CFS consultation held in February 2000. Initially, CFSCC advocate input was sought and included. Regrettably, confusion arose when the focus of the meeting evolved from informing the CFSCC on the current state of the science of CFS to a "think tank" model of NIH consultation in which the primary objectives were to ask acknowledged experts in related fields to take a fresh unprejudiced look at how real progress in this area might be best facilitated. This revised approach was shared with the CFSCC during an NIH report at a November 1999 meeting. Another concern was that an internationally recognized NIH researcher in the area of CFS was included in the February meeting even though he had recently concluded his CFS research program. However, the organizers thought that such an individual would be highly appropriate to provide an overview of where CFS research has been and a personal perspective of what opportunities may lie ahead.

Finally, the Department is pleased to note that the GAO recognized our most recent efforts in fostering better interactions among the members of the CFSCC and within operating divisions. Further, it is evident that the operating divisions are moving into areas of research endeavor that bring state of the art approaches to the study of CFS and

2

that appropriate oversight of CFS research programs is now in accordance with Federal requirements.

3

GAO Comments

1. Our draft report acknowledged that agency officials told us that communication between agency scientists occurs on an informal basis and that much of the research funded by the agencies is extramural in nature. Moreover, we did not question whether CDC or NIH officials communicate with each other. Rather, we reported that we found no evidence of collective research resulting from this informal communication.

2. We noted in the draft report a number of misperceptions that patient advocates seem to have about the work at NIH. For example, regarding patient advocates' concern about the lack of research on mycoplasma, we note that the agency has not received grant applications on mycoplasma; therefore, NIH is unable to fund such work. We also note that the agency has not disproportionately funded research on issues related to CFS and mental health.

3. We noted in multiple places in the draft report that only one planned study—on CFS in adolescents—was not initiated by CDC because of insufficient funds and that the agency later determined the study would be infeasible. However, CDC now has activities planned in at least five areas, using $12.9 million the agency is providing to replace funds previously redirected. This suggests that had those funds been available at the time they were budgeted and had adequate planning occurred, these activities could have been initiated earlier.

4. There is no objective way for either NIH or us to know how the use of a special emphasis panel to review grant applications has influenced the scoring and funding of those applications. We have added to our report that agency officials believe that review by the special emphasis panel improves the chances that a grant application will get a fundable score.

5. The state of the science meeting was originally discussed during the April 1999 meeting of CFSCC and was planned to run in conjunction with the fall meeting of the committee. According to documents we received, meetings began in August 1999 between agency officials and a patient advocate member of CFSCC around planning the state of the science meeting. In October 1999, members of CFSCC were informed by the executive secretary of the committee that the state of the science meeting would not take place at the same time as the fall committee meeting because many of those who were invited were unable to attend on the dates selected. The October communication

also indicated that members of CFSCC would be informed as soon as a new date was selected, presumably so they could plan to attend the meeting. While the meeting was briefly discussed at CFSCC's November 1999 meeting, the draft minutes of that meeting do not make clear that the meeting would no longer be public. It was not until December 1999 that an agency official reported to a CFS professional association that the meeting would not be open to the public. It was some time later that CFSCC members were invited to observe the meeting. However, they were not consulted in the agency's decision to shift the focus of the meeting from informing CFSCC on the current state of the science to an NIH CFS consultation. The draft report notes that CFSCC members raised concerns about the participants in general as well as a number of specific participants invited to attend.

rdering Information

The first copy of each GAO report is free. Additional copies of reports are $2 each. A check or money order should be made out to the Superintendent of Documents. VISA and MasterCard credit cards are accepted, also.

Orders for 100 or more copies to be mailed to a single address are discounted 25 percent.

Orders by mail:
U.S. General Accounting Office
P.O. Box 37050
Washington, DC 20013

Orders by visiting:
Room 1100
700 4th St. NW (corner of 4th and G Sts. NW)
U.S. General Accounting Office
Washington, DC

Orders by phone:
(202) 512-6000
fax: (202) 512-6061
TDD (202) 512-2537

Each day, GAO issues a list of newly available reports and testimony. To receive facsimile copies of the daily list or any list from the past 30 days, please call (202) 512-6000 using a touchtone phone. A recorded menu will provide information on how to obtain these lists.

Orders by Internet:
For information on how to access GAO reports on the Internet, send an e-mail message with "info" in the body to:

info@www.gao.gov

or visit GAO's World Wide Web home page at:

http://www.gao.gov

Report Fraud, aste, or Abuse in deral Programs

Contact one:

- Web site: http://www.gao.gov/fraudnet/fraudnet.htm
- e-mail: fraudnet@gao.gov
- 1-800-424-5454 (automated answering system)

United States
General Accounting Office
Washington, D.C. 20548-0001

Official Business
Penalty for Private Use $300

Address Correction Requested

Lightning Source UK Ltd.
Milton Keynes UK
UKOW04f1812260417
299940UK00001B/112/P